I0698724

Finds Your Map

Learn a Methodology to Take your Company to the Next Level of Success.

Faider Andrade Solarte

@encuentratumapa
www.encuentratumapa.com faider@encuentratumapa.com

Summary

I hope this book is a valuable source of inspiration for the reader! Based on personal experiences, where various obstacles were faced both at the business and sports levels, the story offers a transversal methodology. The goal is for each reader to find usefulness in this methodology and feel motivated to pursue their dreams and goals in life. The combination of real experiences and lessons learned provides practical guidance that can be applied to various areas of life. May this story inspire you to achieve success in your own endeavors and goals!

Copyright:

© [2023] by [Faider Andrade]

ISBN: 9798871667835
Label: Independently published

Dedication

This book is dedicated to those who undertake it for the first time, and especially to those who do not give up, no matter how many times you keep trying, since success is in the one who continues in battle, not in the one who is already done. gave up.

Thanks

First of all, I thank God for the experiences he allowed me to live, the staff who worked with me at Launica, the athletes and coaches who were part of this story.

INTRODUCTION 11

PREFACE 13

PART ONE FINDING THE MAP 14

The map search 14

The fact that?' instead of 'How?' 18

The Secret of Setting Ambitious Goals 18

Enjoy the process, have fun 21

The Champions League final has arrived 22

You reach your goal, raise the level 23

The difficulty and the test 24

Despite Everything, Keep Focus 25

In the crisis the opportunity appeared 27

climbing the mountain 29

Going down the mountain 31

The revelation 32

Check the map 33

Learn to read the map 35

Finding a guide or mentor 37

Discovering the waterfall 38

The connection..40

Close the cycle and move on 41

SECOND PART BUILD YOUR MAP 44

How to build the map...44

How to maintain a winning mentality.....................53

How to improve...55

Vision 56

Goals 62

Activities to be executed......................................64

Follow-up..66

Overcome Obstacles and Challenges 68

Cultivate Positive and Productive Habits.............70

Relationships and Support Networks....................71

Celebrate and Learn...72

THIRD PART OTHER MAPS...........................74

Sport...74

From athlete to coach...76

Promoting sport..76

combat sports...77

Ready for the Quadrilateral 77

Hanging up the gloves 78

Coming to Fight 79

Training plan 80

How to be a champion? 81

Forgetting to be champion 87

PART FOUR ON THE SHOULDERS OF GIANTS ..89

4 Principles 89

Business leadership 92

Headhunter and delegate 93

Smith's principles and wealth 97

Vgaf 100

Great businessmen 100

FIFTH PART ERRORS 104

Avoid making these mistakes 104

Blur 105

He makes mistakes 108

Don't wait to know everything 109

Focus on what you want 110

CONCLUSION 112

Introduction

The world longs for stories that emerge from years of diverse experiences, giving rise to notable successes. This book encapsulates a journey that achieved a seemingly unreal milestone: an increase in sales that exceeded 2,000% in just 20 months. By fulfilling this purpose, the goal was raised 10 times more than what was achieved, achieving new ideas to reach the new growth goal.

More than exposing the actions and decisions that led to this achievement, this narrative is born from the responsibility of inspiring managers and entrepreneurs, contributing to the development of their visions and goals.

For the purpose of simplicity, knowledge molded from concepts extracted from various authors and teachers throughout life is presented. This real and practical testimony offers a redesigned methodology that demonstrates that "everything" is achievable with determination.

In the first part, you will immerse yourself in a personal experience: the business journey that begins at the La Joaquina waterfall, in Sandoná, Nariño. After four climbs, you reach this natural wonder surrounded by exuberance. Although the first three ascents were unsuccessful, each one was filled with valuable experiences, comparable to the search for a vital map to achieve great goals.

The second part reveals the application of the Vgaf methodology, key to the extraordinary results narrated here. This acronym, which represents vision, goals, activities to execute and monitoring, is made available to you so that you can apply it in your own businesses and professional activities.

The third part explores other maps and experiences, bringing principles and ideas to the sporting field. The main premise is clear: different maps can lead to success in life.

The fourth part serves as a prelude to a more extensive volume, where learnings from entrepreneurs who have built empires are shared. It seeks to address persistent concerns about why some achieve great successes compared to smaller ventures.

The book's closing focuses on error prevention, offering valuable lessons about how human wisdom lies in overcoming obstacles during expansion.

Preface

It's ten at night, the cold seeps through the cracks in the window. It has been a week since the internal call I had to write this book. Some will believe that it was a call from God, while others argue that it was communication with the other self, the inner being, or that the universe conspired to lead me to dedicate myself to this work.

The responsibility of writing this book became more and more imperative. I could not continue postponing the confrontation with this blank page, looking at the chapters as an insurmountable challenge. Finally, I made the decision and focused on starting to write. What follows is the result of that decision.

At the transportation terminal, waiting five hours for my trip and just two hours away from boarding, I immersed myself in the content on my cell phone. At that moment, a little voice inside prompted me to action. I remembered similar situations in the past, times when fascinating books were lost in the forgotten shelves of my memory.

This time it was different; The various experiences of life had led me to a treasure map. This map, for the purpose of this writing, is intended to guide you to the wonderful treasure that also awaits you.

Part One Finding the Map

The map search

We never know for sure when our search for the map begins. Throughout life, we discover that it is not just about finding one map, but about discovering multiple maps. These maps have the peculiarity of guiding us from point A to point B, from our starting point to where we want to go, tracing the route to a hidden treasure, something we deeply value.

With the acquisition of experience, these maps become more accurate. How quickly you find the map, whether in your early years or after a few decades, lies in the skill we develop, along with your determination and persistence, to achieve genuine goals.

At first, I didn't know I needed a map. It was only in my forties, after participating in ventures where I admit to not having sufficiently cultivated my determination and persistence, that I understood that a large part of my life was dedicated to developing that map. As an expert cartographer, I have been charting my own path to achieve dreams and purposes.

Now, dear reader, you have in front of you a work that I hope will save you time, allowing you to take actions with greater confidence from the beginning. Although my words may sound directed at a young audience, I want to make it clear that this should not discourage those who have passed that stage of life. Great businessmen like Ray Kroc and Colonel Sanders, founders of McDonald's and Kentucky Fried Chicken (KFC) respectively, have shown that age is no excuse. Whether you consider yourself too young, think you still have time, or think you're too old, their stories teach that it's never too late to start a new path to success.

What for some could be a perfect excuse, for others becomes the catalyst for success. The true limitation has always resided within you, as has the opportunity for a new beginning. Right now, experience is less relevant than ever; The crucial thing is to find the map that will guide you towards your goals.

The search began and begins from your birth, and even before, but it is from the moment we begin to become aware that the search for the map really begins.

I started my search at an early age, around eight years old. As the oldest child, I assumed responsibilities in the family business as a child, helping with tasks that were within the scope of my abilities to support my parents' entrepreneurial efforts. This is how my journey in the business world began.

The historical wealth that accompanies your personal history has been fundamental to building your life map. Let me put it more clearly: who you are right now is the result of all your experiences, both positive and negative. Thanks to these experiences, you have become the wonderful human being that you are today.

You have incredible potential that, as you read this book, you will identify with reflection points where you will value the moments of success that you have experienced in your life.

The police officer approaches to ask for my ID number at the terminal, a routine procedure that momentarily takes me out of my thoughts.

This situation makes me reflect on how different periods of life are crucial to building our personal map.

Deep in designing strategies to lead my team to reach the daily goal of $10,000 USD in sales, I began to map out our path to success. Full of joy and motivation for the new partnership we have just entered into, my mind focuses on a clear goal: I was sure that achieving it would take us to the next level. Although at that time daily sales were barely approaching $500 USD and my partner thought that reaching $1,000 USD would be good, in my mind what was brewing was what for some would be considered completely impossible: I was aiming for a 2,000% increase in sales.

The venture consisted of a commercial establishment that distributed more than five thousand different references. It was located in a relatively small town and was just taking its first steps. My inspiration came from the story of Sam Walton and his creation of Walmart, which also began in a small town called Bentonville, in Arkansas.

It is essential to feel gratitude for the achievements of the great teachers who began before you, who led the way. Although the results they achieved seem unattainable, here is an example of how to get closer to them and even surpass them. It all depends on what you really want. In these pages, a method based on real experiences is reflected that can take you very far on your path to success.

This book could be titled 'How to Achieve a 2000% Increase in Sales in Your Business'. Although what you will learn here is completely real, it is natural that you may have doubts before acquiring this skill. However, this skill is fascinating and essential for growth. He is yet to discover how to do it, just like the team he led at the time.

I was talking to the team, and I'm sure they saw me as crazy. I'll probably have to ask them what was going through their minds at that moment. At first, we struggled to reach the goal of $1,000 USD in daily sales. To be honest, I had no idea how we were going to achieve this in a completely traditional business, without the scalability advantages that the internet and other types of businesses offer. We were simply a commercial establishment, like any other in a small town or a neighborhood in the city.

Years of life experiences had led me to believe that I could do it. However, my academic logic did not provide me with a single resource on how to do it in practice. The only thing I knew internally was that I was going to make it.

It was that hunch, that certainty that invades you when you feel that your time has come. I knew it was now or never. Despite having gone through various moments before, this time my energy and attitude were different. I felt like I was creating something great and everything around me took on a different hue. Although the reality was that of a small business, in my mind I was running a large company. Everything was transformed thanks to the power of imagination; In my mind, it was already a reality.

The fact that?' instead of 'How?'

How to achieve it? Early on, I realized that the 'how' doesn't really matter. That's what I've understood over time, and I want you to understand it too now that you're drawing your own map. The truth is that the 'how' is so unimportant and irrelevant. What really carries weight is the 'What?'—three letters with deep meaning for your life. So I invite you to reflect and write: What is the most important thing you want to achieve at this moment in your life?"

Yes, I know, it's not easy at first. Let me develop the idea and you will soon understand. It is a commitment that, with time and determination, you will end up defining the resources necessary to achieve it.

The Secret of Setting Ambitious Goals

Now you may wonder, why set the goal of selling $10,000 USD daily when we don't even reach $1,000 USD in a single day? Let me reveal to you the biggest secret I discovered: setting a goal that high makes getting to a possible point much easier. For both my mind and the team, it was easier to reach $1,000 USD once we focused on visualizing $10,000 USD. It was as if by aiming so high, the path to more realistic goals was cleared of mental and emotional obstacles.

Reaching $1,000 USD was relatively easy, but as we reached that number, joy and euphoria took over us. Five months later, we began to exceed $1,000 USD consistently. Once achieved, it was necessary to stay above that figure, because falling below it was easy and demoralizing. The entire team had been focused on this goal, and supporting their leader in reaching $1,000 USD per day became more real and achievable than $10,000 USD.

At first, setting a goal of reaching $10,000 USD per day, when we knew that we were not even reaching $1,000 USD, seemed almost a mockery. However, as I repeated it with determination and with increasing force, I began to convince myself that I would be able to do it. The surprising thing was that little by little, my conviction began to infect others, and they also began to believe in the possibility of making it a reality.

Daily prayer began to bear fruit when I asked God for wisdom and intelligence to build my goals. That's when I started to change, I went from being a leader with a 'What?' to understand the 'How?'. I started to understand how to do it, because when the 'What?' It's clear, the 'How?' it becomes easier to find.

The word of God tells us in Matthew 7:7, 'Ask and it will be given to you.' This teaching began to make sense in my life as I understood the power of prayer and faith that God will provide the answers to my requests.

The answers or ideas began to arrive at night. The first time an excellent idea arose to achieve my goal was around three in the morning. I remember being half asleep and realizing what a brilliant idea it was, marveling while I was still asleep. When I woke up, I felt certain that it was an incredible idea, but I must admit that I couldn't remember it the next day. As the day went on, I only felt the anguish of not being able to remember that winning idea.

It was the first experience with the idea that came during the night. At dawn, after a few days, another idea arose in a dream and I managed to remember the previous one. Both ideas were exceptional, and in the dream, I firmly believed that I would achieve what I had set out to do. I felt completely happy as dawn broke. That morning, between the anguish of not being able to remember the ideas and the happiness at their brilliance, the process of exponential growth had not yet begun.

That's when I came up with the idea of having a notebook or my cell phone nearby to write down the next idea. I had already lost two ideas that I couldn't remember the next day. I was more prepared for the next opportunity, but again it happened. On this third occasion, as a result of the dream and the dream state, I did not wake up and continued in the dream. The next day, when I woke up, I had the feeling of three brilliant ideas in my mind, but I didn't write them down and I didn't remember what I had thought.

Sometimes, we need to lose in order to trigger the change we seek in ourselves. This transformation process is challenging and comes from within us, with extraordinary strength. When you begin to feel this change, your determination becomes stronger and begins to transform your life completely.

The fourth time turned out to be the charm. From then on, I made sure to meticulously write down the ideas that came during the night, knowing that if I really wanted to achieve my goals, I had to act. It was crucial to not only have the idea, but also execute and put it into practice. I understood that it was not enough to carry out the idea; It was essential to ensure that the idea itself was successful enough to move the project forward.

Enjoy the process, have fun

As the days went by, before starting operations in the business in the morning, the morning meeting was held. This session, which lasted 30 to 45 minutes, had a clear purpose: to focus the team on the day's goal. The notable thing about these meetings was that at the end of each talk a new strategy, idea or action plan was communicated to them. He always concluded with a prayer, expressing gratitude to God and maintaining faith in reaching $10,000 USD in daily sales.

The days passed and it seemed like nothing was happening. The frenetic pace of daily activities sapped our energy. Doubts assailed the team about the possibility of achieving the objective, and this was completely normal. Many times, people around us do not believe at first. Their level of belief is so low that it does not allow them to see what we are building. It is not easy for those who are not in tune with our vision to understand where we are heading. The only thing that is really important is to keep your thoughts and actions focused on achieving the proposed goal, no matter what happens and no matter how the challenges arise.

Over time, applying the ideas with the best attitude and aptitude, the magic began to happen. The group's self-esteem and self-image began to grow, something that at first seemed unattainable became real. Suddenly, the entire team began to believe that it could be possible. The strategies implemented turned out to be a resounding success, and although I do not detail them here, it is important to keep in mind that the ideas arrive at the right time. Reading about Walmart's ideas, strategies, and tactics, I felt overwhelmed. Implementing is not simply about copying; Each situation requires inspiration and thought to solve the challenges that arise.

The Champions League final has arrived

As we implemented the ideas with the fervor we had injected into the team, something extraordinary suddenly began to happen. We felt like we were in the final of a championship almost every day. We maintained constant joy and excitement, backed by faith and confidence in the future. We knew we were making it. There were days where we surpassed $5,000 USD, $6,000 USD, and even reached $9,850 USD in a single day. The euphoria was incredible; Everything was going amazingly, in that business in which not even $500 USD was sold per day.

It took us approximately 20 months to get there, with successes and mistakes along the way. During this time, learning was consolidated, preparing us for the great transformation that was occurring in the company. Reaching the goal is victorious, but nothing compares to the climb when no one believes and you do believe. Day by day, guiding the team towards that goal, with passion and dedication, allowed us to begin to achieve it little by little. The process was as rewarding as the final result.

In the midst of the boiling and effervescence, calisthenics gave me the opportunity to present the new goal to the team. As a leader, I had raised the bar and now it was my turn to raise the team's level as well. It was at that moment when I simply added a zero to the previous goal and set myself a new objective: to sell $100,000 USD per day in a small municipality, with no more than twenty thousand inhabitants.

Saying we did it is important, but in the long run it doesn't teach as much as the process of how we did it. Dear reader, you too can achieve this by finding your own map.

You reach your goal, raise the level

We were close to reaching the goal of $10,000 USD per day, but I decided to raise the bar once again. Otherwise, we would enter a zone of compliance that, over time, transforms a highly productive team into a discouraged and apathetic one. It is our dreams that motivate us, and we dedicate our tireless efforts to building the future that lies ahead of us.

I remember that day when we almost reached $12,000 USD. I smiled and knew that we were about to surpass the $10,000 USD barrier.

In the midst of this chain of thoughts and prayers, we applied the ideas and strategies we had planned. We realized that, with perseverance, we could reach $32,000 USD in a single day. I had never felt such euphoria before, because the strategy I had in mind to achieve this was already clear.

Detailing the strategy to reach $10,000 USD or even $100,000 USD is not as crucial as being certain that your strategies will be just as effective. The mind, when focused or put in "check," will give the ideas as explained with prayer, having faith in finding the answers you really need. Always remember that you are made in the image and likeness of God.

I could tell you about the various emotional states the team was experiencing while we were experiencing this, but I know you will be experiencing them too. You will remember this stage as if you were on my team and I was part of yours now.

They're going to laugh, but you keep going.
They're going to make fun, but you keep going.
They're going to doubt you, but you keep going.
Your partners are not going to support you, but you continue.
Do the work as if it were for God, that's what the word teaches us, and that's how it should be done.

You will live experiences that will make you grow, you will learn and solve problems that will arise. Imagine this: every new solution you find in your life, in your entrepreneurship, will lead you to new challenges. Embrace problems, because the way you face them will determine your growth. He who stands up in the face of a problem defeats the giant, but he who allows himself to be defeated does not succeed. You are the David of your own story.

The difficulty and the test

The despair of not selling, along with the anguish of covering fixed expenses; the constant worry about making payroll and the difficult situation of having to decide to fire people who believed in you and whom you had finally come to believe.

When things are not going well, moods are changeable; Suppliers call and everyone wants money, including you. But in this fortnight you don't get paid either; You haven't been paid for months and the landlord seems to be no longer your best friend.

At all times, and especially in times of difficulty, is when we truly discover who we are and what we are made of. In difficult situations, we decide which version of ourselves we will carry forward: that of a gladiator or that of a coward.

These are times when you most expect support from your partners, especially if it is an organization. To grow, they will focus on finding real solutions. Otherwise, you'll just have a board complaining because they don't see the expected results.

Despite Everything, Keep Focus

Even when the indicators say you are losing, focus on your dreams and goals. In times of adversity, which will always arise, consider that it is just the test that life is giving you to determine if you are prepared for the blessing that is on the way.

A bold mindset is essential to building the foundation for something great. You must scare away your fears and stay away from people around you who make you afraid, even if they are loved ones. It's hard to accept it, but that's how it is. Curiously, the most fearful tend to be those closest to us. In some way, they try to protect us from pain and suffering. However, there are also people who do not want you to succeed, because if you do, they would reveal their own lack of ability. Often, they don't tell you directly, but their actions speak for themselves.

Walking away in terms of what you're doing doesn't necessarily mean breaking off relationships. It just means that some people don't have enough information about your path. Organize your life in such a way that you do not allow information that may worry them to reach their ears. This will not only preserve your mental health, but will also benefit your environment.

If you find yourself in a situation where your partner opposes or completely disagrees with what you are doing, you are facing a very complex situation. Unless the relationship is strong and based on mutual understanding and support, you could face significant challenges.

Problems will always be present; It's something normal. We cannot expect to know everything before starting a venture. He used to be one of those who dedicated his life to learning everything before starting to do it. However, in practice, I realized that this is not a good path. Learning about business in theory without putting it into practice is completely unpedagogical.

Every problem has multiple solutions; just choose the best one. I remember hearing this lesson at a conference a while ago. The speaker shared that it had cost her thousands of dollars to learn this lesson. Now, you too benefit from reading it.

This technology allows you to achieve what you really want in life. Pay attention and focus on this: the most important thing you need is **to SIT DOWN AND THINK, TAKE A SHEET OF PAPER AND A PENCIL** . As strange as it may seem, all we need is to sit down and think and face finding the solution. It's fascinating when you realize that's all it takes.

What do you wish? Sit down and think about how to achieve it. At first, ideas may not flow easily, but this is a matter of training. Every time you try again, it gets easier. Remember that everything is trainable, improvable and learnable. So, go ahead!

In the crisis the opportunity appeared

Now I am no longer a partner, something I experienced firsthand, a situation similar to that of Steve Jobs (proportions kept). I have seen the famous movie about Jobs several times, and I never imagined that I could experience something similar. Knowing that I could somehow experience what he felt and experienced was shocking. I had the magnificent opportunity to experience it, and that's how it happened.

We were excited about the idea of reaching $32,000 USD in one day. Suddenly, the mission was clear and we were ready to spring into action. The joy and euphoria we felt was only compared to what I experienced when I was national champion. The feeling the team had at that moment was truly sensational.

While in this process, I received a message that said: "You don't own anything, you haven't signed any documents." Even though I knew it was, that little voice inside challenged me to prove it, and so I did.

In previous days, that little inner voice warned me about the issue, but I argued by saying: "You don't understand, we have a verbal agreement and I trust this person." There were several thoughts about it, until finally that voice began to have an effect on me. I decided to take the necessary measures and prepare the relevant documents.

I make the unexpected call, the one you don't want to make but you know you have to make. Deciding to do it and realizing that the little voice was right, I entered a state of denial. The first thing I did was personally corroborate this fact.

Many things crossed my mind. I felt used, completely let down and very sad about what I had heard. However, I decided to go listen to it in person. He was furious; It was not the best attitude, but prayer with God little by little calmed me down. As I drove to the verbal confrontation, the planned argument was going to be incendiary. However, as I repeated the talk in my mind during the almost three hours I drove the car, my temperature dropped.

The mind in this situation thinks about many things. The lack of clarity I had in this regard led me to put the handbrake on the strategy. For the first time, I self-sabotaged my conscious life. Feeling this way, knowing that everything you did in 20 months of work, suddenly vanishes and disappears without you realizing it (we reached the goal of 2000% in twenty months), is heartbreaking.

When I arrived, it was calm and collected. During that period of time. I found myself in an unexpected situation: they confirmed that I was not a partner, but simply a salesperson with sales commission. I went from being the owner of the sign to becoming its best salesperson. The news did not sit well with me; It was not the answer I expected nor the reality I had imagined for myself.

climbing the mountain

Climbing the mountain and praying became my personal ritual in situations that required concentration and solution. I was inspired by the practices of the old testament. If you are a believer, I invite you to do the same; If you're not, try it anyway, and you'll see how the solutions start to appear.

"Climbing the mountain and praying became my personal ritual in situations that required concentration and solution."

I climbed the mountain in search of wisdom and answers. At the time, business was at its peak, but I felt like I was building a big building for someone else. Frustration and confusion took over as I searched for guidance high up on the mountain.

He remembered the words of Jeremiah 33:3: "Call to me and I will answer you, and I will show you great and hidden things that you do not know." As I climbed the mountain, I desperately repeated this prayer, crying as if something had broken my soul and I needed to scream to the universe for answers.

As I climbed the mountain, I searched for answers. Although it wasn't easy to understand, I think what I did was cry out. And best of all, I found what I was looking for.

I climbed the mountain for more than three hours, covering approximately three kilometers. As I ascended, I didn't find the answers I was looking for, but I still wanted to find them. The higher I climbed, the closer I got to finding them, although thoughts of emotional despair plagued me.

Suddenly, I came to a place where there was a map that I had seen eight years ago. At that time, I had climbed for the purpose of exercise, but I did not have enough time to reach the Joaquina waterfall. Now, in search of answers, he was determined to reach out.

The first time I went up, about 8 years ago, I went to a certain point and came back due to lack of time. On this occasion, as I climbed, I remembered how far I had come and I was happy because now I was going to see the waterfall. The climb was steep and the higher I went, the more physically tired I became. I hoped to get there as quickly as possible, walking and appreciating the landscape before me.

After several minutes of walking towards the waterfall, I came to another road instead of the waterfall. I saw a house and asked some gentlemen if they knew the Jacinta waterfall (it's actually called Joaquina, but this name stuck more to me). One of them told me the direction to get to it. His explanation was that he had to return a little more than 500 meters, exactly where he had come up.

I didn't understand it. He was tired, depressed and in a bad mood. Being nice was not my main characteristic at that time. I told him: "But the map said it should be here." I had such an attitude that, inwardly, I believed as if it were the Lord's fault that the waterfall was not on the path where I had thought the waterfall was."

Going down the mountain

As I walked down the mountain, I kept thinking about my search and the questions I was asking myself. Despite having gone halfway, he still had not found the answer he was looking for. He doubted he would even find her, especially when he needed her most. On previous occasions, he had found answers while climbing the mountain with a purpose. Now it was different.

Suddenly, I heard a noise in the middle of the jungle. I got closer and the noise increased. I got scared and ran. I thought it was a rattlesnake, but since I had no experience with those types of sounds, I could be wrong.

Finally, I arrived at the starting point where the map was. Unlike the first time I went up, I met some locals who I asked about the waterfall. They pointed me in the right direction to get there and offered me to accompany them. There were three of them, and one had a machete. My self-preservation instinct told me no, so I thanked them and they left.

On the map, which was a sign one and a half meters wide by two meters long, there were some bushes that separated the path I had taken from the true route to the waterfall. I didn't see the real route either the first or the second time I went up. At first, I was convinced that the path I had taken years ago was the correct one, but since I couldn't finish it, I never knew if it really led to the destination, to the waterfall.

Many times in life, we get confused and take the wrong path because we have not completed the processes or closed the cycles. Only when we conclude and close the cycles do we know how far we can go. In the meantime, we will have an empty and meaningless experience that will not nourish our existence. This leads us to go around in life and return to the same starting point.

After saying goodbye to the gentlemen and setting off to go down the mountain, I was smiling. The message and the response had arrived, and the main objective for which he had risen was clear. The message came to me with so much power and forcefulness that I smiled gratefully. He had had the revelation.

The revelation

I was happy and excited, because the message came very strongly and was so clear that my tears were now tears of joy. I felt a relief in my soul and the power of my heart beat in gratitude to God, because I had received the answer. I understood everything and thanked God for everything. Everything that happens to you is for the good, when you learn to see the positive side of things. My momentum was charging again for another start, though I didn't know what. The only thing I knew was that I was better now.

"Everything that happens to you is for the good, when you learn to see the positive side of things."

I understood everything and, thank God, everything that happens to you is for the best. I learned to see the positive side of things and my momentum was being renewed for a new beginning, although I didn't know exactly what it would entail. The only thing that was clear to me was that I already felt better.

I remember a story the church pastor shared. It tells the story of a king and his squire. The king, riding a horse, hits himself with a tree branch. The squire tells him: "Thank God." The king, a little grumpy, looks at him out of the corner of his eye. Later, the king, preparing his shotgun, accidentally shoots it and blows off part of his finger.

The squire says again: "Thank God." This time, the king immediately ordered the squire to be locked up. Months later, some Indians capture the king and plan to make an offering to the gods. When it is about to be sacrificed at the stake, the witch or master of the ceremony checks the offering. Look at the head, arms, abdomen and chest, everything is fine. However, upon checking the feet, he realizes that the offering is defective and decides to free the king for this reason.

Back in the castle, after being freed, the king sent for the squire and told him what had happened, apologizing in embarrassment. The squire, looking at the king calmly, tells him: "No, for everything you have to thank God. If I had gone with you, I would have been offered to the gods. I was always at your side. For everything, thank him bye bye.

This message resonated strongly in my mind and the words amazed me. My enthusiasm grew and tranquility returned to me.

Check the map

The message began to resonate in my mind, revealing that years ago I had not managed to reach the waterfall due to the lack of a map. Although the map was always there, the first time I tried to go up, I didn't pay much attention to it. But this time it was different, now that I had seen it, I understood the importance of the map in life.

In that moment, memories of everything I had experienced came flooding back to me: the successes and failures that had shaped me into the person I am today. I had visualized the goal of selling $100,000 USD in one day thanks to the entire process I had gone through. Meeting this goal and the way to do it became the map I had been drawing over time.

Now I knew how to set big goals in life and achieve them. I understood that the fundamental thing was to know what I wanted to do with my life; the "how" would come in addition. I just had to dare to do it and take risks along the way. Even though I had been building my own business, I had faced legal challenges in the past, something that was not new to me.

Looking at the map, everything became clear. When talking to the farmers, the clarity became even more evident. Now I knew that I could start again in another activity and that on that new path I could draw a new map for myself, whatever industry I decided to focus on again.

The message resonated strongly and everything intertwined in my mind, although capturing that same feeling in written words was challenging. In short, the process to discover how to sell $100,000 USD a day was the fruit of the experiences I had: this was my map and it could be yours too.

On my first attempt to climb the mountain, I didn't make it due to the lack of clarity on the map and the absence of anyone to ask. This led me to the conclusion of the importance of learning to obtain a map with the wisdom and experience that one has at that moment. The amount of experience doesn't matter as much as the action of doing it; Along the way, you learn and understand everything. As we maintain focus, we will develop enough maturity to carry out any project or purpose in life.

"The amount of experience does not matter as much as the action of doing it; along the way, you learn and understand everything."

Everything was clear, at least that's what I thought. I reflected on this truth and realized that I could now create my own map. I realized that I was capable of being the builder of my own maps, designed for my personal use. I couldn't make a custom map for someone else; I would have to know that person deeply to be able to help them. Therefore, I preferred to share this story as an example for those who are ready to chart their own path to success.

The second time I tried to climb, I couldn't make it either. Although I had seen the map, I couldn't understand it and had no one to ask. In some way, this story is my way of listening to you and accompanying you in building your own map to success.

Learn to read the map

The next day, while I was still reflecting on what had happened to me, my nephew arrived, that loved one who came seeking advice in one of the most reflective moments of my life. I told him the whole process and he became the first person to hear this entire story.

Excited, he told me that he wanted to go to the waterfall. I replied: "Come on, I don't know her either." I looked at the clock, it was after two in the afternoon. I did some mental calculations and decided to accompany him. We rode the motorcycle to the point where it could be reached by vehicle, we parked it and I explained to him the wrong path I had taken in my first attempts. With certainty, I told him: "It's this way."

We started running excited to arrive quickly. We continued moving forward, he ran with agility beside me. Later, I realized that he was no longer by my side. I turned back and encouraged him to go faster. We continued running and in our haste to get there, we reached a point where we realized we needed more time. There was a fork in the road; I took the path that went down, but a few meters later I felt lost regarding the waterfall, so we decided to return.

Meanwhile, I received a call from a friend. We talked about business, spiritual growth and other topics. I found out that Mike Tyson had fought again this morning; Although he clearly won, a draw was agreed upon, since it was an exhibition fight. I also learned that Elon Musk had risen to second place on the list of the richest men in the world. I deeply admire these two exponents for their ability to build their own map to success in their respective fields.

Back at the office, we got on the motorcycle and came down the mountain without having seen the waterfall. We didn't have time, but we made a commitment: to write this book. This story had to be told, and so I promised the nephew.

A few days later, I had the opportunity to tell this story to a friend. She, so charming and delicate, listened to me with enthusiasm and followed me attentively while I told her how far the story went. He was moved by the story and decided to accompany me up the mountain to see the waterfall together.

We planned the ascent, but this is already a detail. The important message is to learn how to build the map. Each person must learn to chart their own path, and mentors along the way will help you shorten the process.

Finding a guide or mentor

The following Sunday, after having made a commitment to go up the mountain with my friend and not finding anyone else to accompany us, she became discouraged about going up, so I decided to go up alone. This time it was the charm, the fourth try.

I had a different purpose in mind this time, something that is outside the context of this book. I will only say that my intention received a positive response.

When I got to the point on the map, I started to notice some significant differences. I studied the map carefully and suddenly, a young man of approximately 14 years old appeared. I asked him if he knew the waterfall and he confirmed that he did. The gentlemen on my second climb did not know the waterfall, which taught me the importance of knowing who to ask and what to ask.

I explained to him that on the way to the waterfall there were two paths, one going down and the other straight. He told me to always walk straight and never go down. So I decided to follow his advice and started my journey towards the waterfall.

Discovering the waterfall

The distant sound of a waterfall began to fill the air as he walked further into the thick vegetation. Every step I took brought me closer to the destination, although the path was wet and slippery, and the small streams I crossed wet my shoes. Humidity hung in the air, and the overgrown vegetation indicated that no one had set foot there in years.

After walking for a long kilometer, he finally reached a clearing in the middle of the jungle. Before my astonished eyes a spectacle of nature was revealed: a majestic waterfall, tall and powerful, falling into a natural pool of crystal clear water. But the most amazing thing of all was the rainbow that danced in the water droplets, creating a spectacle of dazzling colors that illuminated the landscape.

I cautiously approached the waterfall, the small particles of water enveloping me. It felt like a gift from heaven, as if nature itself was celebrating the arrival.

Excitement overwhelmed me as I immersed myself in the natural pool. The cold water enveloped him, and the force of the waterfall hit my body with revitalizing energy. He felt like he was in a dream, like he had discovered a treasure lost for centuries.

At that moment, I felt like a true discoverer, like a pioneer who had found a secret corner of the world. Euphoria filled my emotions as I let myself be carried away by the wonder of the waterfall, grateful that I had persevered in my search despite the challenges along the way.

And so, in the middle of the jungle, I found not only the beauty of nature, but also a sense of accomplishment and wonder that would stay with me forever. My heart beat to the rhythm of the waterfall, and his spirit rose with the magnificence of the rainbow.

Looking at the map, I realized that there was another route closer to the road, I estimated it was about 100 meters away, instead of the $1,000 I had to travel where I was going. I understood that the best thing was to learn to read the map correctly and look for the shortest route.

As I walked towards the waterfall, I realized that if I learned to read the map better, I could get there faster. The idea made sense to me. I visualized reaching the waterfall and returning the other side to demonstrate the importance of shortening the path and learning to read the map effectively.

However, upon arriving and marveling at the waterfall, I was disappointed to realize that there was no short route. The message was modified: it was no longer about learning to shorten the path, but about following the map correctly.

In life, we often look for shortcuts and quick ways to do things, not knowing when they will lead to success. In these moments, **determination and drive are what really make the difference between success and failure** . Furthermore, failure, seen as learning, is beneficial for our human development, despite what is thought outside the world of entrepreneurship.

> **"In life, we often look for shortcuts and quick ways to do things, not knowing when they will lead to success."**

If others have already found the way, it is important to learn from their experiences. These are the mentors, people who are already on the path we want to reach. Their stories of success and failure can be a source of inspiration for us. In my case, the map was well done, but assumptions and misinterpretation led me to erroneous conclusions, distorting the true message.

> **"If others have already found the way, it is important to learn from their experiences."**

This experience reminded me of a story about a king who convened a council of wise men to create a document that could guide anyone who read it, giving them control over their destiny. The wise men met for five years and presented twelve volumes on how to achieve this. The king, seeing the books, asked for something shorter. Five years later, they returned with only one book, but it still seemed too long for the king. After another ten years of work, they presented a single sheet on which it was written: **"THERE IS NO SHORTCUT WITHOUT WORK . "**

The connection

The waterfall map led me to understand that for the business I had built different methods throughout my life that concluded in the construction of high goals. And to achieve these goals in the same way as reaching the waterfall, as in a simile, life itself acting as the great teacher that it is.

This simile of understanding the map to reach the waterfall and achieving great goals in business, produced this result.

Close the cycle and move on

The final conversation with the partner, which was not confrontational but more of a gentleman's talk, made me understand the importance of being grateful for everything that happens in life. At the time, you may not understand the lesson God is teaching you, but looking back, I realized that I had earned more and had more free time to enjoy life. This is priceless. The map I was building at the time was on track, and I was creating several maps for myself.

The meeting became a mutual explanation of what each had said, thought and believed. I concluded that it had been a communication problem. He kept the company, I kept the map, and we were both happy with what God had destined for us.

Delving into the details of this story is not the purpose of this book, and it would be unfair to express my position here, since the truth is holistic, and my counterpart is also right in this matter.

Learn to extract the most valuable from life; In every moment, there are teachings of wisdom that the world needs to know, and you can be the teacher that we all need to live better.

"In every moment, there are teachings of wisdom that the world needs to know, and you can be the teacher we all need to live better."

It's time to reinvent yourself once again. You have to maintain a positive attitude, trust in the present and have a clear perspective on the future.

Steve Jobs, after leaving Apple, reinvented himself and revolutionized nine different industries. In the film about his life, he eventually returns. I don't know if something similar will happen in my case. The only thing certain here and now is to face reinvention with passion and confidence in the future.

"In life, we don't get what we deserve, but what we negotiate in writing."

After freeing myself from that situation and with a clear mind, the ideas arrived and creativity flowed. I reviewed the available resources and focused on work capacity. If he had already achieved it once, he could do it again. A true champion must defend his title again and again, as long as he has the energy to continue competing.

"What happens in your mind is more fun than social media"

When you are truly focused on your goals, you experience an internal story so spectacular that it eclipses any external distractions. The fascination with what you are achieving becomes so intense that social networks, platforms like TikTok, Facebook or Instagram, and other forms of entertainment lose relevance. When you get home, when you lie down at night, you close your eyes and immerse yourself in the movie of your life, you realize the incredible thing that is happening.

In that state of concentration, what happens in your mind becomes more exciting than what happens around you. The wonder of your own narrative, of your projects and memories, takes on significantly greater importance than what might be happening on social media, international news, or technological advances. This deep focus on your goals creates an inner world so vibrant and enriching that it becomes a source of satisfaction and meaning, overcoming external distractions.

When you reach the point where what's happening in your life is more fascinating than anything on social media, you realize that you're dreaming at the highest level your mind will allow. This state reveals that you are on your way to achieving something big, something gigantic. This level of focus and dedication is only achieved when you are truly committed to developing your full potential. You are on the threshold of achieving significant goals and achieving extraordinary levels of success.

Second Part Build your map

How to build the map

In the first part, practically everything that happened in a case study that led to success with a 2000% increase in sales in a period of twenty months was detailed. Now, we will focus on building a map, a methodology that can be applied in different contexts and cultures. The objective was achieved, but what is truly essential is to convey to the reader that you can also achieve what you set out to do, achieving what you set out to do is easy, determining that setting out to do is the complex thing and where human beings waste the most time, including the lack of purpose. They end with a life that could shine.

It all starts with an acronym developed from experience, which helped generate clear ideas to teach how someone else can build their own map. This acronym is Vgaf, which refers to: Vision, Goals, Activities to be executed and Monitoring.

These elements are essential to develop a work agenda, the product of a series of plans to be executed to move from point A to point B.

A complete Vgaf takes place over a period of four years, using the analogy of the Olympic cycle. Just as high-performance athletes prepare for their best performance and break Olympic records, in your business and in your life, you will plan to achieve these results in your field. Each year is divided into four plans to be executed every three months, which gives rise to four microcycles in a year, sixteen microcycles in a period of 4 years.

Vision: Vision is a long-term statement that describes the desired future state of an organization, company, or individual. It is a clear and inspiring image of what we want to achieve in the future.

Goal: A goal is a specific, measurable objective that a person, organization, or company strives to achieve in a given period of time. Goals are concrete and set to measure progress toward achieving broader objectives. They are clear, defined statements that describe what you intend to achieve and provide clear direction for action and focus. Goals are achievable and realistic, and are set with defined time frames to evaluate success and progress on the path to achievement.

Activities to be Executed: The activities to be executed refer to the specific tasks and concrete actions that must be carried out to achieve a specific objective and achieve the proposed goal. These activities are planned actions that are part of a process or project and are designed to meet predefined goals and objectives. They can vary in complexity and scale, and are often organized in logical sequences to ensure orderly progress toward achieving desired results. These actions are essential to implement strategies, complete projects and achieve established goals, and require proper allocation of resources and adequate monitoring to ensure their successful execution.

Monitoring: Monitoring refers to the process of monitoring and evaluating progress towards achieving established goals and activities to be executed. It involves regularly reviewing performance, identifying areas for improvement and making necessary adjustments to strategies to ensure progress is being made in the right direction.

In the three-month Vgaf table , there is an example for reference, in the first column are days from 1 to 90, and in the first row are the activities to be executed, at the ends are the compliance percentages, which must be at 100%.

For example , activity 1 was executed daily achieving 100%, the following activities ended with 50%, 30% and 20%. On day 1, the three scheduled activities were carried out, resulting in a score of 75% achievements. This is to be able to carry out daily monitoring of the activities to be carried out. Correct monitoring guarantees that the proposed goals are met and thus the vision. When the proposed activities to be executed are not so effective, they are changed, the important thing is to achieve the goal, better ideas can suddenly appear and if an activity has to be changed, it is changed to meet the proposed goals.

The clear vision or clear dreams of what you really want to develop is the most difficult thing to do in reality, when you achieve clarity in what you want, how, over time it is organized, You do not have to wait to have all the answers at the beginning, at the beginning the only important thing is to be clear about where you are going, after reflections and prayers in faith and gratitude, the most spectacular ideas will arrive.

"You don't have to wait to have all the answers at the beginning"

<table>
<tr><th colspan="6" style="text-align:center">CONSTRUCTION OF THE VGAF MAP IN THREE MONTHS
1/16</th></tr>
<tr><td colspan="6">Vision: Consolidate the distribution company as a national chain, specialized in the retail and wholesale sale of a wide variety of non-food products. With virtual marketing channels to reach a diverse audience and satisfy their needs.</td></tr>
<tr><td colspan="6">Goal: Manage to sell 10,000 USD per day in a town of less than twenty thousand inhabitants.</td></tr>
<tr><td colspan="6">Activities to be carried out:
1-Get 10,000 USD in daily sales.
2-Develop a wholesale distribution channel in 32 nearby municipalities
3-Get 3 suppliers to represent your brands in the region
4-Have 20 clients per month with the Tras Tras Tras strategy.</td></tr>
<tr><td rowspan="2">Day</td><td colspan="4">Activities to be executed</td><td rowspan="2">Yes
Follow-up</td></tr>
<tr><td>1</td><td>2</td><td>3</td><td>4</td></tr>
<tr><td>1</td><td>1</td><td>1</td><td>1</td><td></td><td>75%</td></tr>
<tr><td>2</td><td>1</td><td>1</td><td></td><td>1</td><td>75%</td></tr>
<tr><td>...</td><td>1</td><td>1</td><td></td><td></td><td>fifty%</td></tr>
<tr><td>88</td><td>1</td><td></td><td></td><td></td><td>25%</td></tr>
<tr><td>89</td><td>1</td><td></td><td>1</td><td></td><td>fifty%</td></tr>
<tr><td>90</td><td>1</td><td></td><td>1</td><td></td><td>fifty%</td></tr>
<tr><td>Yes</td><td>100%</td><td>fifty%</td><td>30%</td><td>twenty%</td><td>xx%</td></tr>
</table>

Table 1 Vgaf at three months.

When the What? It is now clear that the only thing that begins to be needed is to determine the step by step, the activities to be carried out, what must be followed.

For this reason, you have to face the blank page and start writing, considering the latter as the maximum technology for achieve everything, now when you are already in execution when you are already thinking about this daily, dreaming of achieving certain results, the key will always be in the prayer that we pray daily, because it is a prayer that we pray with faith and with belief that this is going to be real, that it is going to be possible and within a short time or x amount of time, you have to believe what you are really asking for because we remember that the word tells us "ask and it will be given to you."

When you are in the state focused completely on dreams, there is no reason to be bitter, to be sad or to express any type of negative feeling, but quite the opposite, since you are always focused on practically achieving your dreams or vision. the company, the organization, that is destined to develop and in this case, the focus is simply on working, that little by little the ideas of that or those objectives of what needs to be achieved, will be achieved little by little. little by little.

While you remain in the state of expectation, in this state in which you are visualizing what you really want, the energy is completely positive, the energy is pleasant, the energy radiates to the work team you are leading. It's great because everyone around you will see hope that you are absolutely clear about what you want, and how it is going to develop, or the key ideas, the key strategies to get there, little by little they arrive. In the example, the goal was achieved in twenty months, it does not mean that the brilliant idea arrived at the end of this period, no, the brilliant idea arrived in the third month, and as it arrived, it began to be executed.

The execution of the Activities is a supremely important part, because if there is a brilliant idea, the million dollar idea, but if nothing is done with that idea, then nothing is going to happen because the only way, the only really important thing It is that it can be done, execute the ideas that will come to mind, with the right mentality and attitude. If these ideas are worked on with the team, the work team has to give them enough energy, enough information so that they become empowered with it and make the idea flow, as if it were theirs to understand it, to understand it, to make it flow. adopt following the instructions of their leader.

At first the ideas came like three in the morning, completely asleep, resting and I did not imagine that in this way the best ideas were going to arrive so early in the day. How he didn't write them down, he didn't write them, when he woke up he couldn't remember what the idea was, in the middle of sleep it was a little difficult to get up to take notes, to be able to analyze the idea in the light of day. This happened exactly on three occasions, the idea came, I thought it was great and the next day or trace of what the idea was, it wasn't until I decided to start writing in a notebook and my cell phone next to me, to make the respective notes. .

Obviously nothing happened if I didn't write them down first, and if I didn't write them down then there would be less execution of that idea, so over time I simply thought about how good that idea was but that I didn't do anything and it was sad, very sad because I was left with the feeling that it had been a brilliant idea that I had had, at night sleeping and some call it the subconscious mind, but we believers know that it is God who begins to manifest, and begins to give us the key ideas that in order to achieve what we have really proposed. It is also true that ideas can come at any time, I have experienced both being asleep and being awake.

Why let's remember and remember is very important, for a moment start thinking that you are managing a company, that company does not sell more than $500 USD a day, but the focus on that company moving $10,000 USD a day, when you are not even reaching at $500 USD.

This is not going to be found in academia, in technical books, in planning, because simply, the 'correct' thing is for one to have a growth of 5%, 10% from year to year, or suddenly a little more than 20%, but growth like the one achieved requires another type of knowledge, it is exponential growth, completely unrealistic. Even the way of writing this cannot be, let's say, with any other basis than the narration of something that happened, which there is not the slightest doubt, that if it is implemented in another context, in another culture, in another company, with another idiosyncrasy, it will always and when the fundamental principles that are being transmitted in this chapter can be implemented, it is completely certain that you can obtain the most incredible results, that you could never have imagined, where one ends up saying, "because I didn't dream bigger."

So what remains is to implement the methodology well, which is a simple methodology, which could easily make it more complex, and which for the methodologist is satisfactorily adequate, and many times we fill entire books, and the complexity of the pages makes whether it is written and then forgotten or not used, it is simplicity as seen in table 1, what it seeks is to focus on what is important in a single glance.

The tools necessary to achieve great objectives are clearly defined with the acronym Vgaf, and the key to this process is REPETITION . Note that at the beginning, although the goal was high, over time and the clarity of the organization's purpose, all They focused on getting it.

It was repeated daily to the work team, with the execution of the activities, the confidence and security that it was going to be achieved grew, the results after months of trying were giving the expected result. Those who saw that it was crazy when I prayed in the mornings, asking with faith and gratitude because these are not normal things, this is not normal that when you sell less than $500 USD a day, you want to get to selling $10,000 USD so quickly, much more so when you reach $10,000 USD, the new goal of raising the barrier to $100,000 USD per day was set, because a zero makes or contributes and allows you to completely leave the state of comfort and not settle for less, if there is the capacity only It is a matter of setting the goal and starting to work for it.

A reflection, what would have happened if the focus on reaching $1000 USD or maybe $2000 USD, I would surely be pivoting between $1000 USD and $2000 USD, which would have been good, I am not going to say no, the break-even point We reached it with $850 USD, so selling between $1000 USD and $2000 USD was good.

If the approach had been less demanding, the ideas and execution could also have been less demanding in their application. The energy it transmitted would have been different and this is where we have to be clear with entrepreneurs, it is very different when you are pushing an ice cream cart selling on the street, if you go out to push that cart knowing in your mind that at the time you will to having, for example, a thousand ice cream carts selling in different cities of the country, the attitude is different, and the level of effort is to such a degree that at the time you are going to want to tell that story.

The people who listen to you, the people who see you, the people who already see you succeed will want to know what you did, how you did it, some will never believe that you started from scratch, but the truth is that in the As you practice, as you do this type of planning, because it is a planning that is done every three months, better said, you get an idea, you execute it, and it is completely established in your daily work, and you continue along the way. next idea and the next improvement and the next improvement, and if you go from improvements to improvements, the time will come when the great goals set will become a reality.

But now imagine this, there is the person pushing the ice cream cart and the only goal he has in the day, the only goal he has in the morning is to get something for lunch, the goal of the afternoon or suddenly to pay for the public service. , then he comes out in a bad mood, says why this company fell to me, that is why there are no more opportunities, he comes out denying life. He comes out denying the situations that are happening to him, he is not looking at the whole picture because the vision that this person has is a vision that will not allow him to grow, but if he knew, he would dedicate himself to using this methodology or a similar one, One day he will be able to have a company with a thousand branches for example, how proud and happy and his self-esteem through the roof, thinking about continuing to expand or in another business, in another industry, the principles are the same.

How the self-image is raised, how that momentum is triggered, if this person believed that he was really going to achieve it, because the only reason why he is not going to achieve it is because he has not set his mind to it because of the vision he has.

Achieving these magnificent results, then, is nothing more than focusing on achieving these types of results, following the methodology that is possible, and here we are to achieve great goals.

"He didn't know it couldn't be done, he just did it."

How to maintain a winning mentality

The winning mentality is acquired by always focusing on the vision we have, not the burden we carry. We must always focus on the vision, on the dream we aspire to achieve, and not on the workload, physical or mental exhaustion. Keeping our focus on where we want to be and what we want to achieve will give us the energy to work hard and consistently when our mind is fresh and in a positive thought cycle.

It is completely normal, since we are humans and our emotionality experiences rhythms that can positively or negatively affect our daily activities. Over time, these rhythms can disperse, allowing procrastination to set in and any obstacle to divert us from the true goal. It's easy to work when we are excited, focused, or when everything is going well in our lives, but right now I must be clear: we must get used to working no matter what is happening around us.

Situations are going to exist for everyone, and what we really need is to focus on what we want. Hard, constant and tireless work is essential. You need to develop such resistance that practically nothing will bring you down: not the breakup of a love relationship, not any situation you are going through, not the painful moments you may be experiencing. Staying firm in the face of adversity is essential to achieving your goals.

We cannot wait for everything in our lives to flow in the best way to begin to act, undertake and climb the mountain of our most desired dreams. You can't wait for everything to be perfect. Even in the moments of greatest adversity, in the midst of pain and difficulties, if you find yourself in one of those moments, first, understand that you are not the only one. Let me tell you, if you focus, you will be victorious. Don't let situations bring you down.

Connect with yourself and look for all your energy in the dreams you want to fulfill. Imagine how you will feel when you achieve those dreams, how you will smile even in the midst of adversity. I remember, for example, the movie "Miraculous Hands", which tells the story of Dr. Ben Carlson played by Cuba Gooding Junior. Despite losing his own children at a difficult time in his life, the film highlights the doctor's attitude, willingness and service to fulfill his mission, facing adversity with courage. Attending a birth.

I don't know if this is a general rule, but when you decide to do something big, you will face obstacles.

These obstacles can hold you back or become steps you climb on the ladder to success, like climbing a mountain. If you manage to overcome every problem, every inconvenience and every situation that arises in your life, you will have reached the wonderful world of human growth.

If you don't let any obstacle knock you down, you'll be prepared to face every challenge that comes your way. Every time you overcome one obstacle, another may arise, but by overcoming it, you will be preparing yourself for bigger goals and more incredible dreams. If you allow the first obstacle or situation to knock you down, this indicates that you may not be ready to face greater challenges. Overcoming obstacles is a decision, and the choice you must make is to move forward, advance and consolidate everything you want and possess.

Along the way, there will be people who are by our side from the beginning, others who appear on our path when we are already building what we want, and there will also be those who we do not even know yet. Some will believe in us, while others close to us may doubt. However, the crucial thing is not that they believe in you, but that you believe in yourself. Focus on what you really believe you can achieve and convince yourself of what you are and what you have. So keep going and don't get discouraged by anything.

Action cures fear, inaction feeds the paralyzing fear that does not allow us to move forward, instead of staying still, act, when adversity visits you, know that it is only a test that you will also pass. Review your dreams, pray to God that everything will be possible for you.

How to improve

Absolutely, that's a valuable perspective. The idea that everything that is measured can be improved reflects the essence of continuous evolution. As a civilization, there has been a demonstrated constant ability to improve the ways in which we perform our tasks and how we approach challenges. Measurement and evaluation are essential tools for this continuous improvement process.

Vision

How to improve vision? How to make the vision transcend? How to make the current vision of the business exciting and stimulating, encouraging continued growth and constant development of the company? The central question is how to make this vision absolutely clear, so that everyone working in your environment feels that positive energy of contributing to something great.

The key is to work on something big and innovative. It is necessary to be so convinced of the vision that, when sharing it with the team, they feel part of something significant and transcendental. A fundamental secret in human relationships is that we all seek recognition.

So, the question arises: What is better? I told them, work as middle management in a large multinational company or collaborate under the leadership of someone willing to reach the big leagues? Everyone responds enthusiastically: 'Sure, we want to get to the big leagues.' Because, ultimately, it is crucial to learn how to inspire our team.

When you hire personnel, you are not only acquiring labor, but also the intellect and emotionality of each individual. In fact, the latter constitutes the most fascinating leverage resource that can be accessed, especially when it focuses on developing the capabilities and potential of collaborators. It is in the emotional sphere of the staff where truly fantastic results are unleashed.

To build an extraordinary team, it is essential to learn to work with individual capabilities and, before that, refine and clarify the vision. It is crucial that each team member is integrated into a specific purpose that transcends the individual parts, thus generating a much greater impact.

The vision that is projected of the business or the activity in which one is involved must be contagious. Employees should feel extraordinarily happy and honored for having had the privilege of knowing you and working with you, considering themselves one of the most outstanding businessmen. No one aspires to work with those at the bottom, as those who do are simply waiting for the opportunity to move to another company. Even the top talent in the market is attracted when the focus is on having a crystal clear vision.

An exercise recommendation in this regard would be to consult the biographies of prominent professionals in the same field. For example, if you are a doctor, explore the biographies of renowned doctors; If you are an engineer, immerse yourself in the experiences of outstanding engineers; and if you are a lawyer, learn more about the leaders in the legal field. In every profession, there is a 'big league' or 'Champions' in which to compete. Every field has top competitions and competitors, and it's essential to explore who those top leaders are in your league for inspiration and guidance.

It is essential to identify who is currently at the top in your professional field and understand the reasons behind their relevance. Investigate their achievements, right and wrong decisions, as well as their training process. In commerce, for example, meeting notable figures like Walmart's Sam Walton can provide a valuable source of inspiration.

If you have already studied a field and discover that it is not your best option, do not hesitate to look for other alternatives and possibilities. Biographies offer an excellent source of information to sharpen your vision by providing a deeper understanding of the path followed by those who have reached the top in your area of interest.

The phrase, **"ON THE SHOULDERS OF GIANTS"** , is truly powerful. Attributed to Isaac Newton, it encapsulates recognition of the greatest minds that have preceded your field. This expression symbolizes the idea that our knowledge and achievements are built on the contributions and solid foundations laid by those who came before us. By recognizing the greatness of those who came before, it highlights the importance of learning from the experiences and successes of those who paved the way, thus allowing knowledge and progress to continue to grow. It is a reminder of the intellectual debt and respect towards those who have left a legacy in the discipline we pursue.

Studying the work of great minds in a specific field is crucial to understanding their contributions, identifying where the frontier of knowledge currently lies, and determining how to make the next quantum leap. Analyzing their achievements sheds light on the innovations and discoveries they made. By understanding the evolution of knowledge in that field, opportunities can be identified to contribute significantly.

The goal is to transcend existing limits and move towards new frontiers. This approach not only involves absorbing current knowledge, but also questioning it, exploring unexplored areas, and seeking unexpected connections. By doing so, a unique and profound vision can be forged in one's preferred field, charting a path forward that not only builds on what is known, but also seeks innovation and progress. This process of study and reflection is essential for those who aspire to contribute meaningfully and creatively to their respective fields.

Indeed, as an example: the child who aspires to be a soccer player is very pertinent. In the field of football, the biographies of the best players offer a rich source of learning. By studying the experiences of the top 10 footballers, the youngster can gain valuable lessons about discipline, dedication and the challenges they faced in their early careers.

These biographies not only provide insight into the tactics and technical skills they developed, but also the mindset and approach they adopted from an early age. Young people can learn about the importance of hard work, overcoming obstacles, and perseverance in pursuing their goals.

In short, studying the biographies of great footballers not only inspires, but also provides practical guidance for developing skills and building a winning mentality from an early age. This shared knowledge can be a valuable source of motivation and guidance for aspiring footballers.

Developing business vision is a fundamental process for long-term success. Benchmarking is, without a doubt, a valuable tool in this context. There are two specific types of benchmarking that can significantly contribute to vision formation: Competitive Benchmarking and Generic Benchmarking.

Competitive Benchmarking: It involves studying and analyzing the practices and results of direct competing companies in the same sector or industry. It allows you to identify the strengths and weaknesses of competitors, understand market trends and discover opportunities for improvement. This approach helps the company strategically position itself and differentiate itself from the competition.

Generic Benchmarking: Focuses on comparing internal processes and practices with companies in other industries that exhibit best practices in specific areas. Facilitates the identification of areas for internal improvement, promoting efficiency and innovation. By adopting best practices, the company can align its processes with its strategic objectives, thus contributing to the long-term vision.

Both benchmarking approaches are valuable for developing business vision. By learning from the competition and internally evaluating the most effective practices, a company can adjust its strategic and operational approach to achieve a clearer vision aligned with its long-term goals.

In the case of a prestigious surgeon, for example, it is about finding the best in the field and comparing all the results. The difference in approaches can lead to mutual improvements. By analyzing your studies, processes and procedures, as well as the challenges you have faced, you obtain a roadmap that indicates which aspects can be improved to achieve high levels of excellence. The doctor can be compared to Boeing company, Google, Amazon or Apple. Benching with a great company can catapult your business or profession to new levels.

What is the legacy you would like to be remembered for? This question, posed in a seminar context, helps the vision acquire the imprint of transcendence.

If you are in any type of business or industry, the process is exactly the same: the comparison, the definition of where you want to go and the beginning of refining the idea. It is crucial to establish and describe the vision with absolute clarity. At the same time, it is essential to have the ability to persuade the team and the people around you, those who believe in you and watch you daily, that you are the ideal leader to take them from point A to point B in a period of time. certain. This given period of time becomes the window in which the company, enterprise or profession can achieve something really big, something of real importance.

I have had the opportunity to work with both professionals and people who are not. From my experience, I can affirm that when a leader has absolute clarity about the direction he is taking, the staff around him begins to work in an extremely interesting way, generating outstanding results. This phenomenon is amazing, since it allows the entire transformation process of an individual to be carried out to reach their maximum potential. It facilitates personal growth, expansion and continued development, encouraging each person to become greater in terms of self-esteem and self-image. This translates into a team that cares about constantly training, that contributes ideas to simplify tasks and that boosts efficiency in a surprising way. Everyone becomes an integral part of the vision, contributing to a proactive and collaborative work environment.

Remember that everyone wants to be next to the winner; Nobody aspires to be part of the last company on the list, but rather the first or the one that aspires to be. Deep down, all human beings want to be part of something great. Sometimes, we already find ourselves within a renowned company, but on other occasions, we have to enter and work with dedication, contributing so that the vision of the company with which we collaborate achieves greatness. It is about trying hard and infecting the staff around us so that they also contribute to the growth and greatness of the company.

With these ideas, you will be able to glimpse the direction in which to take the company or the profession. What is the next step? It can be an expansion in the market, greater product innovation, the search for new and better suppliers, or even the exploration of a new line of business. The key is to carefully evaluate the opportunities and challenges that arise, and make strategic decisions that are aligned with the vision and growth objectives you have set for yourself. This process involves extensive analysis and detailed planning to ensure successful execution of the next phase of development.

Finally, what is your vision? What is the legacy?

Goals

Goals are perfected with experience and time. As we learn to set lofty goals, our being and all our inner potential begin to work in harmony with those aspirations. When goals are low and insignificant, we lack the energy and drive to accomplish them.

Generally, we want our goals to be realistic; However, this book suggests something different: that goals must be completely unrealistic, almost impossible. As the popular adage goes, we must aim for the moon to reach the mountain. The truth is that only when we focus on achieving what seems unattainable and pursue it with determination, are we able to achieve it. By moving towards what is difficult, what seems realistic becomes easy to achieve. When we set goals that seem impossible to most, and still achieve them, we experience something wonderful: we begin to grow as human beings.

Goals must be unrealistic in nature and must be continually adjusted. When we reach one goal, it is crucial to set the next one. In the example we've explored throughout the book, the first goal could have been $1,000 USD, $2,000 USD, or $3,000 USD, but it was ultimately set at $10,000 USD. When we got close to that number, the unrealistic goal was immediately raised to $100,000 USD. Surprisingly, the ideas that emerged to carry out these activities focused on reaching sales of $100,000 USD per day. I even figured out how to make $32,000 USD in one day.

This implies that if our goals in life are modest, the ideas generated by our mind, by the human brain, will also be limited, destined for small things. It makes no sense for the mind to generate the idea of selling $100,000 USD daily when the real goal is $1000 USD. In terms of time, we all have the same twenty-four hours a day, with the majority spent resting eight hours and having sixteen for our daily activities.

The difference in results between people lies in the level of goals they set. Therefore, it is essential to learn to set completely unrealistic goals from the beginning, despite the common notion that goals should be realistic. Only by surpassing goals that seem unattainable does one gain the authority to say: 'If I could do it, you can too.' It is crucial to understand that achieving an unrealistic goal takes time. This aspect of time is what I have shared throughout this text, and if it had taken three times as long, it would still have been worth it.

Activities to be executed

The activities that must be carried out are ideas that may arise on a day-to-day basis. The initial ideas you may have to achieve your goals will evolve and improve over time. During the initial ideation process, it is possible that in as little as eight days, and even less time, in the middle of the month or two months, the activities necessary to meet your goals will undergo modifications or complete certain aspects. As you progress, generate new ideas in the set of activities to be developed, and each one of them is fulfilled. If you form teams to execute them, you can consolidate human talent without needing your constant presence. By forming groups oriented to specific objectives, each team responds to an established objective. Strategies and ideas emerge for execution, and as you put them into practice, you perfect the new ideas.

One of the secrets I discovered and understood was the power of prayer to God. At first, the ideas that emerged did not allow for sufficient growth, but over time, great ideas began to arrive, mainly at night, very late. These ideas were what caused the great change. Initially, I would have burned myself out trying to come up with all the ideas that I eventually executed. From my own experience, I know that those ideas will come. The only crucial thing, what made the biggest difference in the process, was having absolute clarity about my direction and what I needed to do. The dream or vision was to establish a company with a national presence. However, the first goal I set for myself was to sell $10,000 USD a day, an ambitious goal. He knew that if he could sell that amount in a town of less than twenty thousand inhabitants, he was destined for great things. Set big goals in your mind. When you achieve them, you wonder why you didn't set out for something even bigger, and that's the point.

Imagine for a moment that all the great ideas will come to you at once, how difficult and overwhelming it would be for them all to arrive at the same time, the resources and the ability to execute it would be very overwhelming, which could even generate a desertion of intentionality. Therefore, the ideas, as they are executed and perfected over time, arrive in the gradual measure of what you need, this measure of perfection, I don't know exactly what it is like, but I saw that it works. On day one, not all the ideas arrived, nor on day twenty. During the entire period, the best learnings that worked were arriving.

So ideas will come, they will flow, and proper execution of each one is crucial. It is not enough to simply tell the work team what to do; It is necessary to lead by example, inspire and show that the idea works. Sometimes, even if you explain the idea to the team, they may not fully understand it. Therefore, it is vital to constantly monitor: How is it going? What do you think of the idea? Are they executing it? What challenges have arisen? Faced with these emerging problems, it is essential to provide solutions immediately. Everything must flow and consolidate gradually to achieve those great ideas that you are really looking for.

Now, take the time. Many times we underestimate the work that can be done in 20 months and overestimate what can be achieved in a week or a month. When talking about lofty goals, it is common to be misunderstood, thinking that they can be achieved in a short time. I want to be very clear: ambitious goals take considerable time to develop. To set high goals, you must generate a set of diverse ideas that will allow for multifaceted action. This process involves attacking all fronts and evaluating which is the best idea. It's crucial to sift through and determine who on your team can execute it most effectively. This discernment is key to carrying out and realizing those ambitious goals.

Follow-up

Surely, you can write the complete VGAF model. When you have finished it, you will say to yourself: 'I did it!' and you will experience a feeling of satisfaction. You will feel joy in having a clear, brief, understandable and manageable mental map. The ideas flow. Up until this point, this whole thing could have been an academic exercise, and you could have gotten a perfect grade on a spreadsheet from your first three-month planning. You could have even extended the planning to a full year, although I don't recommend it. It is necessary to give time to your mind, your work team and your connection with God so that you can generate the best ideas. The follow-up you give to the ideas you have already had is crucial to provide daily feedback. You set out to sell $10,000 USD in one day, and what happened today? You sold $400. Well, let's move forward with the next idea and strategy, without getting demoralized and avoiding negative thoughts. Constant feedback is essential for continued success.

Negative thoughts are harmful and tend to appear when you least expect them. It's sad, but it's the reality: negative thoughts can turn great ideas into huge shelves that we can't even see, being relegated to the cemeteries of the ideas of men who may have been great in various fields. Many of them did not have access to a methodology like the one the reader is exploring at this moment, a methodology that gives them the certainty and security that, if they focus and determine, they will be able to achieve success.

So the key right now is to accurately determine and track what happened each day and week. Who is getting stronger from the idea? Who on the team is committed to the idea? How can I improve the idea, which is already in practice? Is idea four generating the expected results, or even exceeding expectations? Now, how to take advantage of this new knowledge to perfect the other ideas? Also, it is essential to identify the resources necessary for each idea, since each one represents an activity that must be executed. Often, one can have a great idea but not execute it, and that is where the opportunity is lost. The key to success in this job, if you ask me what is most important, is daily follow-up. Every morning, take a moment to review your vision, goals, activities to execute and the results obtained. It's not just about doing it, but about making sure that the results obtained are aligned with expectations. If you achieve this, you are on the right path to the success you seek.

Also, learn to delegate. Involve your team in the entire process, allowing them to understand and join in the monitoring. It teaches the methodology so that they can carry out their own monitoring and learn to do it with each other. Ask your team: 'How's strategy number one going?' or 'How did strategy number two go?' Explore their experiences and challenges. It encourages feedback between them, generating a dictionary of objections to manage the different reasons why customers may reject a product. This dictionary is the log, the organizational knowledge and the wisdom that your team accumulates to face various strategies. Investing in the constant training of your team to improve their strategies creates a consolidated team, ready and willing to address future goals and strategies.

Finally, it should be highlighted and put in bold because this is the most important thing: **FOLLOW-UP** . If there is no follow-up, everything remains nothing more than an academic exercise, a job in which you invested time, a day, an hour; You created something beautiful on a blank sheet of paper, but if you don't follow up on it every day, if you don't think about it daily and if you don't pray to God with thanks and faith, asking Him to help you, bless you, enlighten you, give the wisdom and intelligence to carry out these ideas, the result may simply be different.

Overcome Obstacles and Challenges

As a general rule, when human beings set themselves great challenges and goals, they will always face obstacles. The best way to address these obstacles is to understand that they will be present for everyone, there will always be challenges. Obstacles can be compared to a series of ascending steps. Each obstacle overcome, each challenge resolved, not only allows you to move forward, but also contributes to the growth of self-esteem, self-image and credibility with yourself. In this way, each improvement pushes you to continue growing.

Henry Ford: Faced technological and financial challenges when introducing mass production of automobiles; Steve Jobs: Overcame adversity and early failures to transform Apple into one of the world's leading technology companies; Elon Musk: Has faced numerous challenges leading companies like Tesla and SpaceX, from production issues to technological challenges in space exploration; Jeff Bezos: Built Amazon from the ground up, overcoming financial and operational challenges to make it the e-commerce giant it is today; Walt Disney: Faced numerous failures and financial difficulties before establishing the entertainment empire that bears his name.

Defining obstacles is recognizing that all of us, at some point in our lives, will face constant challenges. The key lies in overcoming them on our route. It is like a high-speed train that encounters stones in its path; If the strength and power of the coal that feeds your chimney is sufficient, the obstacle will simply be overcome. When the dream and vision of your company are clear, obstacles technically do not exist. Rather, they are opportunities for improvement and growth, teachers of destiny who teach us new skills and abilities that we need to develop. Looking at obstacles positively allows us to see them as allies in our growth. We should never see an obstacle as the end of the road; rather, they are there to push us to grow. No one can be exempt from obstacles or challenges. Therefore, it is essential to develop emotional intelligence to survive them.

In the business world, there will be financial, sales, production, legal, and many more obstacles. The list of possible obstacles is endless, but by seeing them as growth opportunities for us and our team, each challenge becomes an opportunity for organizational knowledge to grow and open the doors to great results. So, if your purpose in life is to grow, welcome to the fascinating world of overcoming obstacles!

If you look at the scene of the largest companies in the world or even at the professionals who have reached the highest peaks in their fields, you will realize that the only difference between them is the number of obstacles they have faced. Obstacles are races meant to polish your character and hone your skills, as well as the skills and character of your team.

Cultivate Positive and Productive Habits

In that methodology, the daily habit of praying, the daily habit of reviewing the plans and vision we have, and the daily habit of repeating the mission or goal that I have to accomplish. This goal becomes an obsession, thinking about it every day, keeping the mind and team focused on how to achieve and exceed. Nothing is useful if we do not set a goal and do not think about it again until 6 months have passed. With this methodology, the idea is to review the goal daily to get closer and closer to it, remembering that dreams and business vision are achieved by going deeper into daily goals.

In this methodology, four microcycles are generated per year, leading to sixteen microcycles in four years. This abundance of plans and executed activities can allow great results to be achieved through continuous, persistent work without giving up. Although the activities to be carried out may change over time, the goals must remain constant. The goal must have an exact date to be achieved, and obsessing about it, thinking about it constantly, even at bedtime, can generate spectacular ideas to achieve.

In the process, it is essential to change the goal once achieved to avoid complacency and continue moving forward. The methodology is based on moving from point A to point B, filling and spreading positive habits, such as daily monitoring of your progress. Charting and reviewing your goals and vision sheet daily will give you a mental framework that you like, reminding you of where you want to go. Faith in yourself and trust in God are key to maintaining energy and the belief that you will achieve what you are proposing. The methodology seeks to establish positive habits that allow you to build and build what you propose.

Relationships and Support Networks

It is extremely important to build relationships and support networks throughout your journey. Along the way, you will realize that contacts are essential to reach clients, suppliers and new opportunities. The people you know can become drivers and promoters of your businesses. Learning to connect positively with them, making a good impression, is crucial for them to become true support networks that help you consolidate your business and project.

They contribute with their knowledge and experience. For example, if you have the opportunity to speak with a successful entrepreneur and present your project to him, in a few words he can provide the guidance you need. Sometimes all we require is a word of encouragement or wisdom to overcome obstacles and grow faster. We live in an interconnected world, where infinite intelligence develops daily. Collaborating with brilliant minds generates incredible changes in the world.

It is essential to learn how to connect with the best in your field and others. Exploring new ways of thinking and seeking inspiration in different areas can drive the growth of your company or organization. The Bible, for example, is a wonderful book that contains immeasurable wisdom and transcends all ages and challenges. Connecting this wisdom to your company's challenges and obstacles can provide valuable guidance in all stages and spheres of your organization.

Celebrate and Learn

It's crucial to remember the importance of celebrating successes, no matter how small. Don't forget to celebrate each achievement, congratulate your team and become their biggest promoter. Also remember to congratulate yourself, especially since you will face challenges when aiming for big goals, as proposed in this book. The process of achieving ambitious goals involves hours of reflection on how to overcome obstacles and consultation with professionals from various fields. With each achievement, give yourself the space to reward and recognize your effort. In the case of writing a book, every page advanced is a victory, so constantly congratulate yourself.

Cultivate your mental attitude and strengthen your self-esteem. Don't let anything bring you down. Learn to accumulate learning from each failure. Life is testing you, and every obstacle is an opportunity for personal and human growth. See how many personalities and companies have emerged in times of great pressure. For example, Gabriel García Márquez conceived the idea of "One Hundred Years of Solitude" on a trip to Acapulco and locked himself away for 6 months to write it.

By asking yourself key questions, such as what you can do and what you are good at, you can discover your true potential and focus your energy towards development. Great examples, such as Jeff Bezos and Elon Musk, demonstrate that building on the foundations of human relationships, contacts and friendships is essential to achieving business success. The construction and construction on these bases are key elements that have brought these entrepreneurs to the top.

Third part Other Maps

In this section of the book, a brief anecdotal introduction is presented that seeks to illustrate how the application of the success principles, previously explored in business roles in the first part of the work, can also generate outstanding results in completely different contexts.

The way events unfolded could be considered another way of discovering or constructing the map. This story was developed thanks to reading "The Magic of Psychotropic Power" by Robert Stone.

The book highlights three crucial elements to achieving anything in life. First, it takes commitment, especially to yourself, about what you really want to achieve. Next, suggest committing to someone else, so sharing your goals will cause you significant shame if you don't achieve them. Additionally, it emphasizes the importance of constantly repeating the desire or goal you seek. Finally, he points out that it is essential to put in the work necessary to make it a reality. With this context in mind, I am ready to share how this philosophy contributed to an interesting sporting feat in my life.

Sport

In 1997, newly arrived in the municipality of Quimbaya in the department of Quindío, he was 18 years old and had been national and international runner-up in

Olympic wrestling two years before. At that time, my greatest desire was to continue my career in sports.

The change of city was due to my father's work issues. We experienced the first financial bankruptcy in the family, liquor and careless management of businesses in the hands of unsupervised employees led us to the point of having to sleep in the van, with our home economically destroyed. It was a challenging period for all of us.

Faced with the family crisis, my parents chose to move to this municipality, motivated by the presence of my mother's niece as the only link to the change of municipality. When I learned about this decision, I was determined not to stay in a place where I couldn't train my sport. I had in mind to return to Pasto and continue my training in case I couldn't do it in the new department.

At this age you believe that things are done the same way as you are used to. When I arrived, I contacted the departmental sports entity to find out the location and training times.

The first reality that I needed to accept was that the training place was an hour away by inter-municipal transportation, and well, who could afford these expenses? If we were just recovering from bankruptcy.

I went once by bicycle, believing that I could continue training in this way, but after two hours on the one-way trip, I understood that the investment of the four hours of which two of them had to be at night, had been spent. ruled out in my recent plan. The training was three days a week: Monday, Wednesday and Friday from

6:00 to 8:00 pm, I used to train in the previous gym from 4:00 to 9:00 pm, it was another complex change.

From athlete to coach

I don't remember how, the president of the Sports League Don Ibert Naranjo and the departmental coach Jorge Barón decided to start a sports process in the municipality, and in their plans was to appoint me as a coach, it was the first job I got different from the family business.

With the new position, I prepared to do what a coach is supposed to do, form the sports clubs to form the sports league, the red Olivetti typewriter began to work, typing with both hands with the middle finger. -I had received typing classes at school, but indiscipline did not allow me to learn much, the only thing is that I ended up forming three sports clubs, - and I convinced acquaintances over 18 years old to be part of the clubs. , I needed 15 people per club, and I don't know how but I achieved it, and the clubs were formed, typed by me.

Promoting sport

With the position in mind, the promotion continued, I went from room to room in each school in the municipality, promoting sports, there I began to make myself known in the municipality, and in this way and with six sheets or soft mats, I He started sports activities in Quimbaya. About 45 enthusiasts for learning came to the call.

Seeing these results of the call, the president of the league managed twenty-one modules of two meters by one, in a cassata material suitable for falls, and they provided me with a yellow tarp, the municipal mayor's office had already given me a space, and Everything was ready to start.

With great enthusiasm at three in the afternoon we began the training that lasted three hours. The children were very happy, they were of different ages, the youngest were the Mosquera brothers, who were aged 5, 7 and 9 years. The potential in them was evident. He was around my age, around 17 years old, and that's when classes began to take place. Now you may ask, what did he teach?

combat sports

In my training as an athlete, we spent around four years training as a wrestler, before my first competition. But the beginning of sports was first with soccer at about 7 years old, a few days after having the guayos I gave up.

A client who frequented the restaurant (a family business), who was a boxer, a dark-skinned man of approximately 1.90 tall called 'Palomo', whose nickname was in honor of the soccer player "Palomo Usurriaga", decides to invite me to boxing classes at the coliseum. Sergio Antonio Ruano.

Happy in my new sport, I practiced it with great dedication at the age of 10, I remember in physical education classes at school, that the teacher, for some reason , made me do the warm-up in his class, and I remember putting my classmates through throw the ya and the hopper while we ran.

Ready for the Quadrilateral

I had been training with dedication for a couple of months, and between shadows and hitting the punching bag, it occurred to me to ask the question: Teacher, when am I going to fight in a Ring? I already knew how to put on the bandages and breathing with the mouthguard was no longer a problem, I already wanted to know the date of my debut.

The professor listens to me, sees me, and with his hands clenched on his waist, he leans down taking a breath, and lets out a laugh. I think I remember it even with tears from laughing so much. said, just the funny moment that I imagine he had.

Hanging up the gloves

The next day I didn't want to go back and I didn't train boxing again, I decided to leave practically "humiliated", I don't remember having spoken to anyone about my decision, I just made it, I walked away and I haven't told this story until now.

The teacher was a very good coach, he brought out several national champions, and he trained one of the great boxers of the time in Nariño Newton Villarreal. With a little more tact on the part of the teacher for me, 10 years old, it would have been a different story that was written here, if it was written at all.

First boxing fight

We studied at the same school with Newton Villareal, at Roosevelt School, and because of the fame he was already gaining, he knew how to bring boxing gloves and headgear to school. Three years had passed since my final retirement from boxing, but boxing haunted me.

In higher grades, there was a student called 'Duck', he was one of those short boys, who everyone respected him because he had acquired a skill in street fighting, and it was Olympic wrestling.

One day the Duck was wearing gloves at school, while Newton was promoting a competitor, I saw that no one was getting into the ring. With a considerable age difference, there I was, determined to enter with two months of classes, "something" I knew, I decided to enter to try real combat.

The fight did not last long, and if it were not for Newton, the fight would have ended in a knockout, with this server on the floor. I remember that I received a flurry of blows from ya to my face, and the only thing I did instead of defending myself was hitting with the same intensity in cross blows, at the same speed, both of us hitting each other at the same time in a frenzy.

I must admit that Pato was the fair winner in this boxing match at school. After knowing that it was about wrestling, I decided to convince my friends on the block where I lived, along with my two brothers, and tell them to come with me to learn about wrestling, which was a gym diagonal to boxing, I knew the way perfectly.

Coming to Fight

We arrived at the gym, and to the surprise of the 7 of us who were going to the gym, a young man two years older attended us, who very kindly invited us to continue to the wrestling gym, and trained us for the first time. The coach friend, one of the greats of Nariño, Jhon Jairo Barbosa, who assisted us, had been training for approximately two years.

I remember that after the exercises, the gymnastics and the technique he made us fight among ourselves, then he fought with us. That day I remember that it was a great day for me, I beat all my friends, and even Barbossa, although writing these lines it is very possible, and I think it was, my new friend, simply let himself win, so that I feel the enough motivation to continue training.

Three years later I am on my way to the first national championship in Palmira Valle. I decided from experience not to ask again, better, when was I going to a national championship? I didn't even know they existed, I just trained and had fun. We had a coach every time they paid him, the rest of the time the more advanced ones did us the favor of training us, and so without a training plan, we did what we believed we had to do to be good.

Training plan

The way the veterans taught us was, one hour of bleachers, one hour of gymnastics, one hour of technique, one hour of wrestling and one hour of weights. Generally we did this every day, and that was the preparation, to get to the weights, there was not much energy but something was done.

This was what I came to develop in teaching, I had not prepared myself to be a coach, nor did I know who to ask, but the desire to continue in the sport made me start teaching.

How to be a champion?

Already in the position of coach, training a team, athletes learning, everything he had done so far. I remember that I just wanted to go to train, but to do so I needed to be a coach, everything I had to do was not programmed in my mind, I just wanted to train.

The announcement of the next championship arrives, three months to prepare, I have no coach, I have no sparring partner of the same weight, I have no one to teach me, I have no books, nothing in my favor, only one coach at one hour and the other at hour and half. I'm alone, I only have the memory of a book I read a long time ago, The Magic of Psychotronic Power.

"When you have nothing else going for you, all you have is the only thing you need."

When you have nothing else going for you, all you have is the only thing you need. In the book I understood three important things: first, define what you want; second commit to achieving it; third, constantly repeat what you want.

"Solving my first map"

The fact that? It was already clear, he wanted to be national champion. Clear and concise as it should be, determine What do you want?

Commitment, the book was very clear that the commitment had to be with myself, and with a respectable or admirable person. The first person to whom I promised to be a national champion was my Aunt Ofelia. She is one of those aunts who were always helpful and concerned so that one could get ahead, she extended her hand to us when things were bad financially. I had no way to repay him for everything he had done for us, so crying and in gratitude, saying goodbye to the new home, I promised him. I felt a very great strength with this commitment, by then I didn't know where I was going to go and what I was going to find.

In the new home, I didn't know who exactly to make this commitment with, so I decided to also do it with the municipal mayor and with the athletes I trained.

When I went to get engaged to the mayor, who was going to be national champion in the next championship, I felt what the author needed someone who follows his lines to feel. The commitment I had acquired was so strong for me that the obstacles of not having a coach, sparring partner and a suitable place to train did not exist, nor did I think about it, until after I had managed to reflect on the matter, and even decades. after.

Because of "mouth", I think I managed to think or maybe I think about it now, the commitment was already made, and I couldn't back out, my entire reputation was at stake, and everything depended exclusively on me. Without sufficient knowledge or experience, I set out to do everything within my power.

I did everything I remembered about how I had to train. Something I did to gain strength, it was a game called, everyone against the coach, and all the athletes came against me to knock me down, and I didn't let go, this became a key routine of preparation, I had nothing else to do at the time.

In the commitment, Stone highlighted that it had to be with that person, that if you see them again in your life, you would be ashamed to tell them, I came second or I lost, you should feel that shame of not making it.

The third thing I remembered about the author was that one had to repeat it daily and at all times. I had thought of several phrases to repeat at all times, these were: I am going to be champion and I am going to win. I decided: **I'M GOING TO WIN** . It became my battle cry. All day long I repeated it to myself, when I trained, when I bathed, at meals, before going to bed, when I got up, on the bus to the competition, at all times.

I repeated several hundred thousand times, I don't remember how many, in the competition when the winds of fear came, I repeated the phrase to myself, in the warm-up I also did it, at all times, the only thing I repeated to myself was this.

The day of the competition arrived, nerves accompany the process, but the phrase "I'm going to win" scared them away. On the day of the competition, an experienced coach was in my corner, Professor Jorge Barón, who led the sport and founded it in several departments, who formed one of the most successful quarries of athletes in Colombia in his lifetime, and his pupils continue to give. great results, now as coaches.

First fight I'm going against Valle, Quindío against Valle, a five-minute fight. I remember a very strong fight, the feeling of fear and nervousness that is felt when the call "Andrade for Quindío, get ready" over the loudspeaker, **I AM GOING TO WIN** , I had to repeat it and it worked, one phrase reminded me of the whole purpose of why I was there.

Next call "by the department of Quindío Andrade", the day had arrived, the preparation was aimed at that special day, that competition, I walked towards the mattress and repeated to myself **I AM GOING TO WIN** , I had to do it, I had already developed the habit of repeating it constantly.

Entering the mat **I'M GOING TO WIN** , looking at the referee, the opponent, listening to the loud bar of Vaaaaaaaalleeeeee, it echoed in my ears, but the loudest voice in me was **I'M GOING TO WIN** . We greet each other and are in position to start the fight **I WILL WIN** .

The whistle blows, what I longed for had begun, **I'M GOING TO WIN** , starting the fight, a very strong opponent, **I'M GOING TO WIN** , what a powerful phrase, without this mental method Valle would have won, I don't have the slightest doubt. From the beginning I got the score back, it was a very even fight, at the end of the time I won by one point, 5 to 4. My coach in the happy corner, and his son who was the departmental coach who participated as a national judge, approaches me and He tells me: "We are now third." There were 4 of us in competition, I won one fight, in my accounts I lost two more, I finished third.

When I warmed up I repeated the phrase I'm going to win, when I entered the mat I repeated the phrase, during the fight I was only focused on winning, in the crucial moments of winning or losing, an internal strength came out, I didn't want to feel the shame of saying to The mayor I lost, she gave me the strength not to defeat myself. Sometimes you don't lose a competition, you let yourself be defeated, and this phrase I'm going to win and this method didn't let me give up.

Next fight, Valle goes with Bogotá, in the stands I looked amazed at the fight, the one from Bogotá, he beat up, the one who had cost me so much work to beat. Immediately the fears that I could lose when I played Bogotá began to appear. **I WILL WIN** .

Quindío against Bogotá, the phrase was repeated to me and it took me away from the cycle of thoughts, in which I had seen the previous beating. There was a part of me that thought I had lost the fight, but the phrase, a lot of phrases, filled me with courage, I warmed up and entered the mat.

Enter, and finish the fight so quickly that I couldn't understand why Valle's competitor was defeated so resoundingly.

Next fight, Antioquía against Valle, the fight was similar to the previous one, Antioquía beat Valle very easily again. Once again those thoughts come, the toughest in the category has been Antioch. Again the phrase; **I'M GOING TO WIN** , to get my mind in tune and move on to the final.

The Final Quindío vs Antioquía

The same process, constantly repeating what was in my mind, constantly repeating my desire, the phrase " **I'M**

GOING TO WIN" served me a lot in this tournament, it chased away the natural fear that one feels when entering the competition.

Already on the mattress, I applied a throwing technique, and my opponent was left flat (both shoulder blades on the floor of the mattress), already on the floor and unable to defend himself, he decided to bite a part of my upper pectoral, close to the shoulder so that Let it go, squeeze it harder, and win the championship.

To this sporting experience, I must add recognition to the family of Risaralda fighters, the three Echeverri brothers, and Jorge Baron father and son, who behind the scenes provided their best support for this process.

Years later I met a friend from the Valle team, who told me that after losing the fight with me, he became demoralized and he had planned to win, when he saw that he could no longer, he was not interested in the podium, he went out to compete. for fulfilling the duty of not physically abandoning, because morally he had already abandoned the competition.

taekwondo

I did the next similar experience using this methodology in Taekwondo. I was in university, and I had to take a sports credit out of obligation, look what there was, and the closest thing to Olympic wrestling was taekwondo.

I always wanted to practice this sport, the monthly payment did not allow me to get started, although if I had asked dad I would have surely paid when I was a child, the truth is I never told him, I assumed he would not pay. My father just liked me to focus on work.

Already at the university, I entered classes, the first day the coach interviewed me and apart from another Karate classmate, he told us if we wanted to go to an open national martial arts championship. In boxing I asked when and the teacher laughed, in wrestling I didn't ask for more than three years I went to the first one, and in taekwondo in the first class they were already telling me when to debut.

I told him: "Surely you think I can go, if I don't know much about this subject." The coach told me, you know how to compete, it's the most important thing. Fifteen days after my debut, he explained to me six key kicks, the defenses, and since he only trained on Saturdays, and I had already committed, I started training at home, at night.

Already in the classroom, I told my classmates, they all started laughing, thinking that they were going to give me a tremendous beating. I didn't like that, so I repeated the method again, the What?, it was already clear, the commitment was with my classmates, I didn't want them to make fun of me in class, and I already had the phrase, it wasn't if I didn't. repeat this that I had already done.

Arriving at the competition, with the direct elimination method, I won the three or four fights, and there I arrived with my trophy to show my teammates. The three of us who represented La Gran Colombia University returned as national champions in our respective categories.

Forgetting to be champion

Before this championship, and after it, in the sport of Olympic Wrestling, I was not national champion again, I reached the podium, but I was not able to repeat the feat of being champion. (In the fourth part of this book I explain what happened).

Later I had great national coaches, who took care of technique, tactics, strategy, physicality, but none of them worked on the mind again, and since I was with those who knew, I forgot this map, I forgot this way, I didn't pay attention to it again. , a "momentary" method had arrived in my life, and just as it arrived it left, and I did not seriously remember this matter again until 26 years later, writing this book.

Part Four On the Shoulders of Giants

In the second part of the book, a method is shared through which it gives a few insights into how to perfect vision. And although there is no university that has the exclusive title of "Improve your vision to a record" or something like that. And it is certain, as was seen in the third part, there are many ways or forms to do it, and here we share another way to reach your true purposes.

In this part, then, it is appropriate to look at those **GIANTS** , from whom we can learn, learn from those who are at the forefront and "copying" what they did is wise, although culturally it seems that we are predestined to believe that copying is bad.

You could say that copying exactly is not possible, but if it can give you a clear idea of how they did it, and how you could do it, or how you can do it better, Hombros de Gigantes is based on the fact that only We manage to do great things, when we understand the work of those who preceded us, it is to climb the ladder of knowledge in the field to continue advancing. It is not starting from scratch, no, it is moving forward, the progress of civilization as we know it is based on this.

4 Principles

The first time I heard about an entrepreneur who owned over a hundred companies, a hundred different industries, not branches, but a hundred completely different companies, I remember starting to pay attention. I began to study and reflect on how they did it. How was it possible for a person with a business to manage such an overwhelming workload? In contrast, figures like Carlos Slim and Li Ka-shing owned 150 and 300 companies respectively. These were giant companies spanning the globe, undisputed leaders in their fields and territories. They had plans for expansion and growth that seemed immeasurable. By digging into these people's biographies, I discovered how they started, how they came about, and what they really did. Knowing the tremendous impact of their achievements is fascinating.

These outstanding entrepreneurs had the ability to discover how to succeed in the markets they entered. They identified the fundamental principles that allowed them to stand out. If a person started a small business, they were often overwhelmed by the workload. Although I had studied two professional courses related to the topic, neither of them provided the exact answer. No one could explain what was happening. In this exercise, I discovered that something else existed, something that escaped my previous studies. If you have been looking for a coherent and logical explanation of how these entrepreneurs have managed to build so many companies in various industries, you have found a book that will provide you with answers and share a meditation on how this can really be achieved.

It is essential to understand that we all have a limited resource: our time, which is reduced to 24 hours a day, less than a million hours in a lifetime. Some entrepreneurs started from scratch, others even from less zero, while some had some initial advantages.

However, what is crucial is the result obtained, which in many cases is immeasurable and colossal. The fact of having started with some advantage cannot be underestimated, since many entrepreneurs have made their name in a notable way, being commemorated, recognized and valued. They have left a mark that lasts and that future generations have learned to appreciate.

During this research, I was able to identify four principles that each of these entrepreneurs began to implement over time. These principles are directly interrelated:

1. Business leadership
2. Headhunters delegate and form teams
3. Smith's principles and wealth
4. Vgaf

To explain methodologically whether what is stated in this part is correct or incorrect, I must be very sincere. Some might argue that the right thing to do is to follow the example of Napoleon Hill, who interviewed numerous businessmen, over a period of twenty years. However, it is also valid to say that you can use your imagination and investigative skills, listening to audios and videos for hours. Personally, I have dedicated extensive amounts of time to listening and understanding, in addition to reading books on various topics, both theoretical and human development.

Similarly to how great thinkers have imagined the workings of the constellations and stars, the process of developing these four principles was an effort that spanned many years. It was a work of reflection, search and constant inquiry, keeping the question persistent in my mind, in order to arrive at these four principles.

Business leadership

Business leadership goes beyond simply envisioning the future direction of the economy. It involves constantly being on the lookout for the next trend, the innovation that will set the standard, or the next market niche to discover.

In this process, it is essential to understand that innovation does not always translate into creating something completely new, but also about reinventing and improving what exists. Take, for example, the case of a restaurant: although the concept itself may not be innovative, the real genius lies in how it is implemented. This is where the business leader demonstrates his or her ability to structure, conceptualize, and execute uniquely.

Foresight, combined with the ability to identify opportunities and adapt to changing market demands, is the essence of business leadership. Thus, a leader not only anticipates the next big trend, but also actively influences how it develops and adapts to it, setting the course for his team and his organization as a whole.

Leading involves entering completely unexplored fields, a type of leadership reserved for those who share the spirit of explorers, who venture into the unknown. This is the leadership of the conquerors, those visionaries who not only create new industries, but elevate them to the next level.

We are talking about the leadership of pioneers, those who invent or innovate, leading the way for the club of true innovators. It is these leaders who challenge boundaries, inspire others to follow in their footsteps, and ultimately transform not only their own organizations, but also the entire business landscape.

Observing what others do not perceive, understanding and anticipating upcoming events is essential. Understanding how major paradigms are constantly changing redefines what is considered business truth today, as well as what works in the business world. New technology and continuous advancements are completely transforming the landscape, demanding a constant ability to adapt to stay current in this constantly evolving business environment.

The city is undergoing a significant change in the way we consume, and in fact, the entire world is undergoing a transformation with each technological revolution. Everything is constantly changing, and understanding, anticipating and adapting to this dynamic is key. A leader not only anticipates, but also documents and trains, thus allowing things to happen both inside and outside his organization. Your ability to proactively lead through these changes is essential for success and relevance in an ever-evolving environment.

Headhunter and delegate

Is people's talent born or created? It is a crucial question, and the answer is that it is born and made, it can be developed, or perhaps its talent already exists at some level. It is essential to take these perspectives into account when evaluating the talents around you. You can discover talent both within your company and in people who are yet to arrive. Sometimes talents are in unexpected places, and exceptional ability lies in transforming an ordinary person into someone extraordinary.

The time may come for every human being to do something extraordinary. This moment is crucial, and it is necessary to carefully observe when it arrives, what is the right moment, what is the exact moment in which life, circumstances and situations lead each human being to offer the best of themselves or to prepare. mentally to do it. It may be that you are at the right moment or that you are close to it, needing that voice of wisdom and encouragement that will allow you to take that big step and develop your potential in an immeasurable way.

These are the keys to starting a new organization or company. There are times when human beings are ready and willing. When we say the phrase 'the time has come', it is essential to be patient and learn to identify how we can ensure that the people who will work with us, with whom we will team up, are always prepared to develop their maximum potential. This is possible as long as we share principles, being essential to move towards an organization that can achieve interesting goals.

Great employers have stood out for their ability to identify and attract the best talent in various fields. True talent has incalculable value, since with it you can start new industries, conquer market shares, achieve significant advances and progress. Finding and retaining this talent is one of the main objectives that outstanding entrepreneurs must pursue. Attending events and participating in various meetings are key strategies, since it is in these contexts where the talent that your company, your business or your next business initiative is looking for could be found.

It could be argued that everyone has inherent potential; However, it is crucial to learn how to properly select talent. It is also necessary to cultivate the ability to empower ordinary people, giving them the degree of autonomy necessary so that they can extract the best of themselves and display the complete inventory of their personal history. This will allow them to successfully take on the great goals and challenges that we set for them, surprising us with their achievements.

In this sense, when discovering various types of talents, it could be argued that the most vital area within a company's departments is the human talent department. This department has the crucial responsibility of selecting the most qualified and exceptional person, since it will be in charge of hiring and subcontracting all the necessary personnel, taking into account current needs, expectations and requirements, as well as future training. The effective assimilation of this hired talent is essential, since it is sought that everyone is completely aligned with what you really want to achieve.

Consolidating an organizational structure based on a broad, abundant and improved selection of human talent is essential. The aim is for staff to constantly feel the desire, longing and fervor to learn and train, continually improving their skills and abilities. In this way, the organization will be founded on leadership that broadly recognizes and values talent. This will allow the company to successfully overcome the various challenges and obstacles that come its way.

Learning to incorporate talent of various ages is crucial, since both accumulated experience and fresh knowledge in new technologies are valuable contributions. The presence of young talent is especially important to take companies to the next level. This phenomenon is evident, especially in technology companies, where it has been observed that it is young people who, with their knowledge of new tools and technologies, have made significant advances and have driven disruptive changes in various types of businesses that have been established. , consolidated and formalized.

When you have experience and are a veteran, it is crucial to invest and reinvest in projects that keep an eye on new innovations. The industry is constantly rethinking, even when there is already a finished and widely distributed product on the market. We know the next big innovation is on the way. Everything is susceptible to innovation; nothing can remain completely static over time. Even in the food industry, over time, products are improved and perfected, along with various forms of presentation and business models to achieve better sales.

Thus, one of the fundamental pillars for building great companies lies in obtaining solid leadership, capable of understanding these concepts and acquiring the best talents available. A great company is built on the top talent available, or those that your leadership helps develop. The objective is that each individual who joins your team feels, in every cell of their body, the impulse to offer the best of themselves, deploying all their capacity to obtain outstanding results, since their time has come.

After identifying and securing talent, the next step is delegation: creating a work plan and assigning responsibilities. It is essential to draw up a clear plan that defines where you want to go, what goals are pursued and what are the executive actions to achieve it. At this point, you can focus on follow-up, especially when it comes to managing a large team, even multiple companies. As the follow-on team expands, it is crucial to delegate efficiently and consider infusing capital, seeking partnerships, and starting new companies in different industries. The correct implementation of these concepts throughout the territory in which you are located is essential for sustained growth.

Providing the foundation for them to learn how to form teams is essential, especially ensuring a deep understanding of this process. It is supremely vital that each new venture has absolute clarity, especially in the area of human talent. This area is responsible for acquiring all the talents necessary for the efficient functioning of your organization.

Now, correct leadership will be accompanied by the best talent, and the best talent will manage to lead organizations to remain on the global podium of business competition.

Smith's principles and wealth

Talking about the principles of wealth simply means referring to the four principles that the illustrious Adam Smith detailed in his renowned and widely cited book "The Wealth of Nations." In this work, which bears the full name of "Inquiry into the Cause and Nature of the Wealth of Nations", the measures that a nation can adopt to become richer and advance in development are addressed in five volumes. Likewise, Smith explores the actions that both a company and a country should avoid to avoid deviating from this path.

In this context, according to Adam Smith, there are four supremely important principles to facilitate a process of advancement or generation of wealth. The first principle is the subdivision of labor, followed by specialization as the second, the construction of tools as the third, and all this must be framed in the size of the public market, which constitutes the fourth principle according to Smith.

The subdivision of labor, according to Adam Smith, completely captivates him when he observes the activity in the famous pin factory. There, he notices that one man cannot produce more than 20 pins in a day, but by having 10 men, each specialized in a specific task, they manage to make 4,800 pins a day. This increase of 460 pins per day for each man was crucial for Smith to foresee the imminent emergence of the industrial revolution. This concept is extremely important for future projects, as it highlights the need to learn to subdivide work.

A correct subdivision of work into various activities, each supported by a specific talent, allows specialization to flourish. When a person immerses themselves in a repetitive activity that demands their unique ability, they can develop a level of mastery and specialization. This continuous, repetitive approach to work leads to constant improvements. In an organization where each individual works in his specialized area due to subdivision, improvement and excellence expand in each segment. This process, from subdivision to specialization, is essential to achieving exceptional performance at work.

Having fully specialized personnel in each area of the business confers a significant competitive advantage. This places the company on a trajectory of continuous growth, achieving goals, meeting objectives and exploring new markets and innovations. Specialization allows each individual to constantly improve in what they are passionate about, which is crucial for the organization to become increasingly competent and competitive.

According to Smith, after specialization comes the construction of tools. He describes the philosopher as one who examines how to optimize the production process to achieve greater quantities in less time, driving significant advances. This approach involves the development of more efficient technological tools, avoiding waste of time. The person specialized in one part of the process is the one who, over time, can generate their own tools as well, an observation that has been confirmed in various industries and sectors.

When these three principles are applied in the context of public market size, for both a company and a nation, the result is considerable exponential growth. The size of the market is revealed to be a crucial factor, since starting a business in a town of twenty thousand inhabitants differs significantly from doing so in a market of 7 or 8 million people. Marketers have learned that market size is fundamental in the creation of wealth. A well-located company, with a large flow of customers, is destined to grow, expand and progress. On the other hand, we have observed that entrepreneurs in areas with potential are often limited by the size of the market, preventing them from realizing their full potential.

An entrepreneur has the full ability to learn to handle Smith's four principles. You are encouraged to understand the size of your target market and hire top talent so they feel confident and realize their full potential. Although the subdivision of work might suggest the need to hire more staff, it is crucial to look at it from the perspective of efficiency and productivity. An excessive focus on subdivision without considering efficiency can lead to a gigantic payroll, counterproductive to growth, since expenses could absorb the profit of the business. It is essential to understand and apply the size of the public market, as explained by Adam Smith.

Vgaf

Learning to guide, to lead a team when everyone does not know the future direction, implies having faith, certainty and confidence in oneself. It requires hard and intense work, but with the conviction that great goals can be achieved. In the model we present here, called 'VGAF', its key lies in focusing on obtaining significant results. By implementing this model, not only are great goals achieved, but the team is also empowered to develop effective work plans. This, in turn, allows monitoring and evaluating individual progress and achievements, constituting an essential element of leadership.

Designing a simplified model that connects vision with action is key to keeping the team focused and ensuring effective follow-up. As could be seen in the first two parts of this book.

Great businessmen

Accompanying the report A Hombros de Gigantes, I share those who without a doubt have been and are great references in the business world, who filled work agendas meeting goals and achieved the dreams or vision they set out for themselves, and serve as an example to generations. of future entrepreneurs.

Henry Ford had the vision of democratizing the automobile, making it accessible to the general public. To achieve this, he introduced the assembly line and standardized production processes, notable with the Model T, an affordable automobile that transformed the transportation industry.

Andrew Carnegie: Andrew Carnegie's vision was focused on leading the steel industry. His goals included dominance in steel production, which he achieved by implementing production efficiencies and acquiring competing companies. Carnegie became a steel magnate and noted philanthropist.

Bill Gates wanted to put a computer in every home. To achieve this vision, he co-founded Microsoft and developed PC software, most notably the Windows operating system. His focus on personal computing and technological development made him a key figure in the technology revolution.

Elon Musk has a vision of facilitating the colonization of Mars. To achieve this audacious goal, he founded

SpaceX, developed reusable rockets and advanced electric vehicles with Tesla. Its disruptive and technologically advanced approach has transformed the space and electric automobile industries.

Steve Jobs, co-founder of Apple, was a driving force in the consumer technology revolution. Their vision focused on creating products that will change the way people interact with technology. With the launch of iconic products like the iPod, iPhone and iPad, Jobs not only transformed Apple into one of the most valuable companies in the world, he also left an indelible mark on the way we live and work. Its focus on elegant design, simplicity, and hardware and software integration defined the aesthetics and functionality of modern technology. Jobs' ability to anticipate market needs and his ability to bring innovative products to the consumer are fundamental to understanding his impact on business and technological history.

Coco Chanel revolutionized women's fashion with the vision of creating an elegant and functional style. Her goal was to establish the Chanel brand, achieved by introducing iconic garments such as the "Little Black Dress." Chanel was noted for its innovative approach to design and elegance.

Warren Buffett, known for his focus on investing and sustained growth, built Berkshire Hathaway. His key success factor lies in a long-term investment strategy and smart acquisitions, becoming one of the richest men in the world.

In this part we could not miss a brief allusion to the most prominent investment funds, which take the entrepreneurial spirit to the highest level, and about whom little is said, but they add important conglomerates in the main markets.

Vanguard Total Stock Market Index Fund is distinguished by its diversified approach, with thousands of companies in its portfolio. Its key success factor lies in offering investors a low-cost investment that tracks indices and provides broad diversification in the stock market.

SoftBank Vision Fund, known for its diversification into technology and emerging sectors, has made a significant impact. Its key success factor is massive financing to high-growth technology companies, supporting disruptive innovations in the global market.

Berkshire Hathaway, led by Warren Buffett, has built a diversified portfolio across several sectors over the years. Its key success factor lies in a long-term investment strategy, combined with Buffett's wisdom in investment selection and business management.

Sequoia Capital stands out for its focus on technology and innovative companies. Its key success factor includes a strong network of contacts and strategic advice, which has contributed to the success of numerous startups in its portfolio.

Tiger Global Management stands out for its global investments, especially in technology and startups. Its key success factor lies in the active search for high-growth companies, supporting ventures that demonstrate significant potential in the market.

Index Ventures has achieved a prominent position with investments in technology and startups. Its key success factor lies in its focus on early stages and close association with entrepreneurs, contributing to the successful development of innovative companies.

Finally, learning from the greats in the field is vital, to climb the next step, and glimpse where you really want to go.

Fifth part Errors

Avoid making these mistakes

Making mistakes is inherent to the process of human growth and learning; They are lessons that polish us over time. The key lies in learning from one's own mistakes and, even more challenging: learning from the mistakes of others, one's own successes and the successes of others.

Learning from successes seems like a completely easy, logical and coherent task. But usually, when things go well, we assume we know why, without truly reflecting on the reason behind that success. In the context of sales, for example, it is crucial to ask whether a sale was successful and, even more so, to understand what elements contributed to that success. By questioning ourselves about what we did well in a sale, we can identify key aspects that led us to success. This constant self-assessment is essential for growth and improvement, as even in a successful sale there are always important areas that can be refined.

Similarly, learning from other people's successes is a complex task. People can often identify that something went well, but it can be difficult to consciously analyze why it was successful. When reflecting on the successes of others, we are faced with the challenge that the person themselves may not have fully understood the reasons behind their success. This process becomes even more complicated when we try to understand the success of companies or individuals at the market level. Concluding what was the success that led to success can be complicated, since even historians or biographers can misinterpret or make mistakes when describing what really happened.

In this sense, understanding and comprehending successes involves delving into the details and consciously analyzing each element that contributed to success. This level of understanding can be challenging, but it is essential to applying meaningful lessons and achieving excellence in any field.

In the hope that these errors will be useful for the reader to avoid falling into them.

Blur

Lack of clarity in vision or sleep is one of the main errors when developing the Vgaf methodology. Without a clear understanding of where you want to go, you can make mistakes in focus and direction. Although it is possible to achieve many things without a clear vision, the end result may not be as desired. The absence of a defined direction makes it difficult to understand the result you truly want in your life. This lack of clarity becomes an obstacle and, over the decades, you may realize that you have not reached the level you want.

It's true that you can reach a level, but sometimes you don't truly realize how far you could have gone. At first, it's hard to imagine how far you can go. For example, when I focused on being a national champion, it was the greatest thing I could conceive of at that time. I didn't consider the Olympics because I didn't even know they existed. An athlete who focuses on national competitions could lose the opportunity to aim for higher levels. This applies to various areas; Focusing on being an Olympic or world champion involves a different mindset and level of intensity, and the work required to achieve those goals is considerable, and we all have the same 24 hours.

Olympic swimmer Michael Phelps, for example, focused on going further and breaking all Olympic records in his sporting discipline. He achieved this goal so outstandingly that he set a very high standard for athletes who follow him, possibly for decades or even centuries to come. Their dedication and achievements not only marked Olympic history, but also illustrate how an ambitious approach can influence the future of a sporting discipline.

Looking back, I realize that this lack of clarity in my vision and goals prevented me from reaching my full potential. I could have given more and achieved much more if I had a clear vision and believed in my abilities from the beginning. This reflection taught me that although we cannot change the past, we can learn from it and use that wisdom to move forward into the future. It is crucial to have a clear vision of where we want to go and believe in our abilities to challenge our limits and achieve great things in life.

It is essential to keep in mind that everything you propose can become a reality if you work constantly and focused on it. However, it is essential to ensure that the goals set are aligned with the result you really want to achieve. That is, your goals should be an accurate reflection of your deepest dreams and aspirations.

Sometimes people achieve extraordinary results that exceed what they originally set out to do. This shows that with effort and determination, you can surprise yourself and achieve more than you expected. On the other hand, it is also possible that you achieve a sensational result that you had not anticipated. This scenario highlights the importance of keeping an open mind and being willing to adapt to opportunities and challenges that may arise on the path to your goals.

Set goals, make sure they are aligned with the result you really want to achieve in life. Remain flexible to adapt to circumstances and be open to surprises that may arise on your path to success. With determination, focus, and a clear vision, you can work toward your goals with confidence, knowing that you are taking concrete steps toward the outcome you truly desire.

Goals become clear when the vision of where you want to go is clear. You can set goals to be a national champion, but also to be a South American, Pan American champion or at different levels of an Olympic cycle. Developing goals that align with the vision allows you to pursue specific results. Whether focusing on breaking Olympic records in your sport or rising above the record in your industry, it's crucial to know what to beat. This is how your name can endure in the universal history of great business innovations.

When goals are rooted in an absolutely clear vision, the activities executed and the ideas you generate to carry them out are completely different. For example, strategies to sell $10,000 USD per day are different from those designed to achieve the goal of selling $100,000 USD per day. The vision defines not only the end goal, but also the nature and scope of the actions you take to achieve it.

What really differentiates one work agenda from another, or one brainstorm from another, is the vision and clarity about where you really want to go. Once this is clear, the key is to maintain proper tracking, as it tells you how close or far you are from the true point you want to reach. In this process, you will notice that as you keep track, you get closer and closer. Enjoy the process, live each day and experience all the emotions that this can generate.

He makes mistakes

It is better to try and make mistakes than never try anything. Avoiding making mistakes can become a destructive brake on the most fundamental ideas. The fear associated with the possibility of making mistakes can be paralyzing. Although there are unpredictable things, if your dreams are clear and the vision is well defined, and you are determined to achieve each goal, any problems or obstacles, even mistakes, will be resolved over time. Action and the willingness to learn from mistakes are essential components of the path to success.

It is essential to remember that we work with human beings, and errors are inherent to our nature. Both your team and yourself will have errors. Being prepared for this means giving them the opportunity to learn from their mistakes. Implementing leadership based on learning through error is key. It allows not only the correction of mistakes, but also continuous growth and development. Moving forward with this approach contributes to an environment where constant improvement is valued and becomes an integral part of the process.

The fear of making mistakes has been the barrier that has prevented many men from conquering the woman of their lives. Many innovative ideas lie buried in the cemetery of oblivion due to the fear of making mistakes. Companies that could have existed in the market simply did not take off because someone at some point was afraid to take the necessary step. This fear can be a significant obstacle, but it also highlights the importance of approaching mistakes as opportunities for learning and growth, rather than definitive failures.

Don't wait to know everything

The desire for perfection is understandable, and we all aspire to do things right from the beginning. However, it is important to recognize that not everything can be learned or mastered immediately. Imagine a relationship, a marriage, or the birth process. You cannot foresee everything from the beginning. For example, telling your partner that you are having twins and going through the pregnancy and birth process involves surprising challenges and changes. Parenting also has its complexities. If we only focus on the problems and difficulties, it would be difficult to take the step towards building a family. But we set out with faith and hope in a better future, without knowing all the challenges in advance.

Likewise, when we start studying, it is impossible to imagine everything that awaits us from the first day to the last, until graduation day. Some fail to finish due to pressure, stress, work, the challenge of pushing one's own boundaries of knowledge, late nights, nights without understanding a subject, and the constant worry of losing a semester. They are difficult processes, but they are part of the path we must follow to move forward. So don't expect to know everything from the beginning. Learning and overcoming obstacles are essential to moving forward. Give yourself the time necessary, everything is a process.

Along the way, you will learn what you need and acquire valuable lessons from great teachers. This path gives you the opportunity to correct and perfect. The fundamental thing is to always maintain a learning attitude, recognize that learning is fun and be in a constant process of acquiring knowledge. Not only will this improve your mood, but it will also remind you that we are focused on the vision we have and what we want to achieve. Maintaining that purpose will allow you to consolidate, over time, what you really want to achieve.

Focus on what you want

The story map in the third part of the book introduces another map that focuses on commitment. In this context, the importance of constantly repeating a "war cry", a mantra that represents your goals and aspirations, is highlighted. In this example, the battle cry was "I'm going to win." The idea is to apply this principle to your company, business, life or any dream you are pursuing. By adopting a rallying cry and constantly repeating it, you tune into what you need to do, giving you constant motivation to move toward your goals.

Instead of focusing on what you want, you make the serious mistake of focusing on the problems that arise. This approach is harmful, since by focusing on problems, errors and shortcomings, we face difficulties. An example of this is when the company was generating less than $500 USD in daily sales, which created challenges paying utilities and rent. However, the mind and energy remained focused on the desired goal, and magically, ideas and positive energy began to flow to achieve the desired result. This story highlights the importance of keeping your mind focused on the goal despite obstacles.

Absolutely true. Focusing on problems weakens and consumes our energy. It can cause us, despite our positive actions, to go backwards rather than forward. Positive attitude plays a crucial role in this process. The daily and constant work, especially in serving our clients, will be reflected and appreciated. Maintaining a positive mindset and focusing on solutions instead of problems allows us to overcome obstacles and successfully move towards our goals.

A beautiful message to close. Always focus on what you really want in the morning, start the day with the best attitude. At the end of the night, take a moment to recognize and congratulate yourself for all the good you accomplished that day. If it wasn't so good, don't be discouraged; Every new day is an opportunity to get back on track towards your goals. Don't give up, keep going, follow the steps learned in this book and I wish you much success in all your endeavors. May the magnificent glory of God our Lord Jesus Christ accompany you forever. Amen.

Conclusion

Just as I began with the first sentence, so it concluded. I must highlight the fascinating journey from the beginning to the completion of this project, a process that has been constantly improving until its completion.

In the first part, a correlation between a business experience and climbing the mountain in search of a waterfall is narrated. This experience was the inspiration to write this book and title it meaningfully. The key conclusion is that any goal one sets in life can be achieved if there is true determination to achieve it.

The second part describes how anyone, regardless of their culture or idiosyncrasy, can develop and take any type of business to the next level by applying the VGAF method, presented in this section.

The third part teaches another method for finding or designing the map, emphasizing the importance of making a commitment to yourself and seeking commitments to an authority that generates real shame or shame if it is not achieved. The importance of communicating your goals is highlighted to keep a constant reminder of why you are pursuing those results.

The fourth part introduces principles that have emerged over the years in response to the understanding of how the most successful entrepreneurs on the planet can run and create multiple companies in different sectors, while an entrepreneur with a single project can collapse from work and stress.

The final part is dedicated to possible errors that may arise. They are presented as a safety net so that the reader avoids falling into them and benefits by anticipating the challenges that may arise when pursuing great goals in life.

In the summary of the book, we understand the seemingly unattainable goals, the focus on big dreams and how, through specific cases, it is concluded that when one sets out and determines to achieve great successes in life, he/she finally achieves them. People don't achieve great things simply because they don't focus on achieving them. When someone is determined to search, scrutinize and dig until they reach the bottom, they can achieve what they set out to do.

We live in a society in which dreams fade as children, being great dreamers, see the abundance of their aspirations diminish. As they grow, education and perceptions change, influenced by the daily experiences and outcomes of those close to us: friends, siblings, family. These results have a significant influence on our own achievements.

If we surround ourselves with successful friends, if we are grateful and bless those who prosper, we are likely to achieve similar results as well. However, often when someone succeeds, society tends to exclude them instead of seeking to learn from their success.

It is crucial to learn to forge and visualize an expansive vision, cultivating dreams and goals that seem almost impossible. Inspiring big goals involves careful execution of activities, followed by proper follow-up. This four-point methodology is simple but is complemented by key aspects such as habit, persistence and values that strengthen human character, such as insisting, resisting and never giving up.

This approach is essential for teaching future generations. Beyond teaching about faith, it is essential to instill in them the idea of pursuing big dreams. To achieve this, it is crucial that your children see you fighting, facing challenges and persisting in achieving your goals. This teaching process not only involves showing triumphs, but also sharing failures and demonstrating that, no matter what happens, perseverance and constant work are essential to achieve what one sets out to do.

Life is wonderful, full of opportunities and abundance for everyone. We can all develop our maximum potential, even the little ones, who can generate significant changes in their lives. Small actions can lead to big transformations.

I congratulate the reader who has made it this far, because he proves to be someone committed, possibly one of those who will send me an email saying: "I made my first plan, I have been there for 4 years, I have achieved such an achievement." I have no doubts about the capabilities; In fact, the certainty that this book will be useful to those who receive it fills me with enthusiasm. I am eager to hear how you apply this knowledge in life and how you pass it on to your children, as teaching these lessons is crucial to passing them from generation to generation.

The great feats in life are the result of people who decided to leave a legacy and do extraordinary things. By setting goals, they were certain they would achieve them, even when those around them doubted. Determination, purpose and disposition are key to achieving great results; Only those who really put their mind to it can achieve it.

It is essential to note that he who has never set out for something great in life will never achieve anything. It is unfair to expect surprising results without preparation or interest. This principle is reflected in inheritances: those poorly prepared to receive them may have a distorted perception of wealth creation. Over time, conventional wisdom warns of the possibility that, after generations, poorly managed wealth will end in difficulties.

Facing obstacles and challenges is a constant in every generation. Only those capable of overcoming them have marked the great advances of humanity. Inheritance is important, but equally crucial is how it is managed and invested. Each generation faces the task of programming and making their dreams come true, learning from previous challenges and projecting a path to success, transmitting this knowledge to the next generation.

www.ingramcontent.com/pod-product-compliance
Lightning Source LLC
Chambersburg PA
CBHW060111260726
48658CB00004B/1506